ANGELS in the OZARKS

PROFESSIONAL BASEBALL IN FAYETTEVILLE &
THE ARKANSAS STATE/ARKANSAS-MISSOURI LEAGUE 1934-1940

also by
J.B. HOGAN

Tin Hollow
Fallen: A Short Story Collection
Bar Harbor: A Short Story Collection
The Rubicon: A Poetry Collection
Losing Cotton
Living Behind Time

Forgotten Fayetteville and Washington County

ANGELS in the OZARKS

PROFESSIONAL BASEBALL IN FAYETTEVILLE &
THE ARKANSAS STATE/ARKANSAS-MISSOURI LEAGUE 1934-1940

J.B. HOGAN

Otterford

Otterford

An Imprint of Roan & Weatherford Publishing Associates, LLC
Bentonville, Arkansas
www.roanweatherford.com

Copyright © 2023 by J.B. Hogan

We are a strong supporter of copyright. Copyright represents creativity, diversity, and free speech, and provides the very foundation from which culture is built. We appreciate you buying the authorized edition of this book and for complying with applicable copyright laws by not reproducing, scanning, or distributing any part of it in any form without permission. Thank you for supporting our writers and allowing us to continue publishing their books.

Library of Congress Cataloging-in-Publication Data
Names: Hogan, J.B., author
Title: Angels in the Ozarks: Professional Baseball in Fayetteville and the Arkansas State/Arkansas-Missouri League 1934-1940. J.B. Hogan
Description: Second Edition | Bentonville: Otterford, 2023
Identifiers: ISBN: 978-1-63373-701-3 (trade paperback) |
ISBN: 978-1-63373-702-0 (eBook)
BISAC: SPORTS & RECREATION/Baseball/History |
BIOGRAPHY & AUTOBIOGRAPHY / Sports

Otterford River trade paperback edition December, 2023

Cover & Interior Design by Casey W. Cowan
Editing by Dennis Doty
Indexing by T. Scott Cowan & Wynnie R. Cowan

This book is dedicated to the late Robert Henry, ex-president of the Arkansas-Missouri League; and to my late uncle, Bob Fultz — the best ballplayer I ever knew and the best coach I ever had; and to all my coaches and teammates in the Fayetteville City Park, Little, and Babe Ruth Leagues of the mid-1950s and early 1960s.

TABLE OF CONTENTS

Acknowledgements ii
Prologue iv
1: Professional Baseball Comes to Fayetteville 3
2: 1934: The Educators 9
3: 1935: The Bears 20
4: 1936: The Arkansas-Missouri League 38
5: 1937: Angels in the Ozarks 59
6: 1938: Hitting on All Six, Mostly 73
7: 1938: Regular Season Champs 89
8: 1940: A Last, Short Season 107
Epilogue 119
Appendix A: League Overview 125
Appendix B: Yealy Champions 131
Appendix C: Yearly League Leaders 133
Appendix D: Yearly All-Stars 149
Appendix E: All-Time Records 159
Appendix F: No-Hitters 165
Appendix G: Major Leaguers 167
Appendix H: Fayetteville Yearly Leaders 175
End Notes 183
Bibliography 191
Index 195
About the Author 205

ACKNOWLEDGEMENTS

I WISH TO express my gratitude to the following people and institutions for their help, support, and expertise in the creation of this work: my late brother-in-law Kirby Estes; Martha Estes; Professor Robert Cochran; Tom Dillard, Tim Nutt, Geoffrey Stark, Ann Prichard, Andrea Cantrell, Cassandra McCraw, and Rachel Reynolds, Special Collections, Mullins Library, University of Arkansas, Fayetteville; Allyn Lord, Susan Young, Marie Demeroukas, Jacqueline Burnett, Manon Wilson and Brenda Smart, Shiloh Museum, Springdale, Arkansas; the late Robert Henry; John Hall; Society for American Baseball Research (SABR); Baseball America; *The Sporting News/Spalding Guides*—(James Meier, Librarian); Pat Doyle; Jerry Jackson; the late Buster Dunlap; Heather Siroonian; Fayetteville *Daily Democrat/Northwest Arkansas Times;* Paula and Judi, Interlibrary Loan, Ft. Collins, Colorado, Public Library; Genealogical Department, Fayetteville Public Library; the late Maude Gold (Mrs. Fred Hawn); Historical Society of Missouri, University of Missouri-Columbia; Longmont, Colorado, Public Library; Ann Sugg and A. D. Poole, Washington County Historical Society. Any errors are the sole responsibility of the author.

PROLOGUE

MANY DECADES AGO, while the country struggled to recover from the Great Depression and as global events moved the world ever closer toward World War II, local baseball fields—like Fayetteville's Fair Grounds park—once rang with the less ominous, though certainly raucous, sounds of professional minor league baseball.

Nearly forgotten now, Fayetteville's team, the Angels, battled other Ozarks teams from Arkansas and Missouri in sometimes remarkable and often rough and rowdy struggles for diamond supremacy.

Few are left now who can recall what it was like to live in Northwest Arkansas in the 1930s. There were only about 7,500 residents within the city limits of Fayetteville—a far cry from today's burgeoning population—and on the mostly uncrowded main streets, which had been paved only the decade before, city car competed with country truck and even wagon. On Saturdays, local farmers came to the town square to sell their produce, visit with one another, and maybe come up with enough change to send the young ones off to a moving picture at the old Royal or Palace theatres.

To the east and north of the square, leading away from town towards Missouri, ran old, two-lane Highway 71. Paved in 1930 to accommodate the incipient triumph of the automobile over slower but less noisy forms of transportation, Highway 71 was a slender ribbon of chalky-white concrete running through the flower and tree-covered hills of Northwest Arkansas.

Though struggling through the Great Depression like the rest of the nation, in those daysFayetteville offered some great deals for folks lucky enough to get their hands on some real cash money. You could, for example, rent a five-room house with double garage for the princely sum of $15 per month, or purchase a "New Bigger" Dodge at McCartney Motor Co. on north East Street for $645.

Opening Day Ad, May 1934: *Fayetteville Daily Democrat*

A dozen "guaranteed fresh country" eggs cost fourteen cents at the Piggly Wiggly and you could buy four pounds of "Pure Hog Lard" for thirty-two cents at The Modern Groceryette on North College—but you had to bring your own bucket to haul it home in.[1]

If you were a kid, maybe you could spend an idle afternoon looking in shop windows on the square, even buy some penny candy at the Scott 5 and 10 Cent Store or take in a free semi-pro baseball game on Merchant's Day out at the Fair Grounds.

If you were unbelievably lucky, you might have been up on College Street one hot August day in 1934 when Max Baer, the heavyweight champion, stopped in town long enough to have his picture taken, joke around with some of the home folks and shake hands with local baseball hero, Fred Hawn.

Fred Hawn
Photo courtesy of University of Arkansas Special Collections Loc. 268

Then again, you might have been hawking newspapers that day: selling the *Fayetteville Daily Democrat*, forerunner to the *Northwest Arkansas Times*, and trying to interest folks in the latest gangster shooting or what commentators like Will Rogers and Mrs. Roberta Fulbright (the paper's publisher and mother of Senator-to-be J. William) might have to say on current issues and events of the time.

In retrospect, the depression era gives the appearance—despite its many difficulties—that for the average American, life was quieter and perhaps simpler than it has become in the decades that followed. But just as no time can be as simple or innocent as nostalgic hindsight would have it be, depression life was hardly easy, most often the very opposite.

It was a time when gangsters and outlaws freely roamed the countryside and when the forces of European reaction inexorably led our nation and the world forward to the massive destruction that would become the "second war to end all wars."

Money and jobs were harder to find than an honest politician, and with local and regional droughts devastating the country's food supply, everyone in those days—from Fargo to Fayetteville—struggled not to just make ends meet, but to live—to eat at all.

Although the realities of the economic depression and the fear of another world war often darkened that distant decade, in the winter of 1933-34 a different, happier kind of build-up was taking place in Northwest Arkansas.

Always a hotbed of baseball, the area had a fine stable of local star players, including Buster Dunlap, Fred Hawn, Homer "Doc" Ledbetter, Jake Drake, and Ike Poole. There were several fine semi-pro teams in the district, including the Fayetteville All-Stars, as well.

During difficult times such as the nation was experiencing in the 1930s, entertainment often provided much-needed relief from the stress of day-to-day living. The exhausted laborer, the unsuccessful salesman, the hungry skinny kid, the put-upon housewife and mother, all of them needed an occasional respite—however brief—from the harshness of reality.

During the warm months of the year, baseball provided just such a break, an escape from the rigors of depression survival. In the fall and winter, there was football and basketball, but in Fayetteville and countless small towns throughout the land, spring and summer belonged to baseball, in those days the unquestioned national pastime.

What Fayetteville and Northwest Arkansas didn't have was actual professional baseball. Semi-professional baseball in the region was excellent without a doubt, but fielding a pro team in a pro league, now that would be something. And the times were right for such a venture.

At its 1932 winter meeting, the National Association of Professional Baseball Leagues (NAPBL), the organization that oversaw minor league baseball, elected Judge William G. Bramham as its president.

Judge Bramham was a man of vision and achievement. When he took office, the NAPBL watched over only 14 minor leagues with a total of 102 ball clubs. When he passed away fifteen years later in 1947, Judge Bramham left a legacy of 52 leagues and 388 clubs. The minor leagues had become a major league success story.[2]

When professional baseball came to the Ozarks, there were five primary classes or levels of minor leagues: AA (at the time just one step below the majors), A, B, C, and D).[3] Normally, because more people typically translates to bigger crowds, thus creating more money for investors and higher pay for ballplayers, the bigger the town, the higher the class ranking.

Geography also played a large part in developing the minor leagues. There were an abundance of leagues in the east, for example, because many of the major league clubs were still located there. In the Northwest Arkansas and Southwest Missouri region, the major league team that dominated was the St. Louis Cardinals.

Branch Rickey, who as a Brooklyn Dodgers executive would later become famous for breaking baseball's color barrier by hiring Jackie Robinson, was a vice-president of the St. Louis Cardinals in the early 1930s. Rickey saw, as did Judge Bramham of the NAPBL, the potential for creating low level, developmental leagues in baseball rich areas like the upper Arkansas and lower Missouri areas. In the winter of 1933-34, a plan for just such a league began to emerge.

At its thirty-second annual meeting, which opened November 15, 1933, in Galveston, Texas, the NAPBL was both expansion- and future-minded. As Branch Rickey would say in January 1934: there "were brighter days ahead for the minors."[4]

With recent improvements in motorized travel, a major obstacle blocking the mobility required to carry on competition between minor league cities had been overcome. Places with natural sporting rivalries, such as the towns of Northwest Arkansas and Southwest Missouri, were poised to make the big leap into organized, professional baseball.

ANGELS in the OZARKS

PROFESSIONAL BASEBALL IN FAYETTEVILLE &
THE ARKANSAS STATE/ARKANSAS-MISSOURI LEAGUE 1934-1940

ONE
Professional Baseball Comes to Fayetteville

FROM SPRING 1934 until mid-summer 1940, Fayetteville's professional, minor league baseball franchise was the only constant in a league that, in its six-and-a-half year run, had teams from nine Ozarks cities and towns—some not much more than communities—in what was once described as the "smallest league that ever functioned in organized baseball."[5]

Originally called the Arkansas State League (it changed to the Arkansas-Missouri League in 1936) and consisting of just four Northwest Arkansas clubs—Fayetteville, Siloam Springs, Bentonville, and Rogers—this Class D circuit came into existence during, and is in fact emblematic of, the extraordinary growth of organized baseball leagues that began in the early 1930s and lasted until the onset of World War II.

On February 22, 1934, the first step towards bringing a professional baseball team to Fayetteville was taken with the arrival of two veteran baseball men and a pair of local enthusiasts. "Red" Wilson and Ed Hawks, each having paid their baseball dues in both the Class A Western League and the Class C Western Association, visited Fayetteville with Charles "Chuck" Morgan, Joplin, Missouri entrepreneur, and Frank "Matty" Mathews of Rogers.

The purpose of the visit was to interview fans and business people on the prospects of organizing a Class D professional baseball league in Northwest Arkansas and Southwest Missouri that would build on already existing support for semi-pro town teams.

A meeting was called for Thursday, March 1, in Bentonville and representatives of Fayetteville, Springdale, Bentonville, Rogers, and Siloam Springs, Arkansas, and Cassville and Seligman, Missouri, as well as officials from any other interested towns, were invited to attend.

The March 1 meeting kept the ball rolling, with Fayetteville's V. James Ptak and Fred Hawn attending. Frank Mathews was chosen temporary chairman and acting-president of the embryonic league. Another organizational meeting was scheduled for Thursday, March 15 in Rogers to discuss the economic realities of fielding a pro team— including player salary limits, renting ball parks, choosing umpires, and "methods of financing" clubs. In addition, J. Walter Morris, promotional director for the Southern division of the NAPBL, would give the new league his organization's clout and support by attending the next meeting as well.

At the March 15 meeting Rogers, Bentonville, and Cassville, Missouri, were ready to pay their $160 league and association dues. Joe Becker, a Brooklyn Dodger scout attending for J. Walter Morris of the NAPBL, told the city representatives that "any city able to take in $600 a month during the three month season would be successful in the league under present plans." As the largest city in the proposed league, Fayetteville was eager to come on board with a team and so, yet another meeting was scheduled for Wednesday, March 21, in Springdale.

In the interim, as Rogers and Bentonville rushed energetically to join the league, acting-president Mathews gave a well thought out and detailed cost estimate for Fayetteville and other club boosters to consider before making their decisions. Mathews suggested the following initial budget for each team:

$30 national association dues
$15 bats
$75 uniforms
$20 baseballs
$15 catcher's equipment
$250 guarantee to league (which could be underwritten, requiring only a cash outlay of $155)

Monthly club expenses Mathews estimated as:
- $25   per player—10 players per team
- $80   per manager—1 per team, usually a player as well
- $36   for baseballs
- $30   for league dues

The grand total: $396 per month. Mathews envisioned minimum receipts as: eight home games per month with a total gate of $160; four Sundays also with a total gate of $160 and two Merchants' Days bringing in $150 for a monthly grand total of $470.[6]

On March 19, Rogers and Bentonville each held meetings and J. O. Clark and Jess Seamster were elected club presidents, respectively, with "Red" Wilson being named Bentonville manager. A call was made again for Fayetteville to join the league and at the March 21 organizational meeting in Springdale, Fred Hawn, representing Fayetteville, said that he would attempt to organize a team and that a "well coached nine that fights every inning" would prove successful. A final meeting was then scheduled for Friday, March 30.

At the last meeting, presided over this time by J. Walter Morris of the NAPBL, Fayetteville—under the co-direction of Fred Hawn and Clifford Shaw—was added to the new league roster along with Rogers, Bentonville, and Siloam Springs. The league would be called the Arkansas State League (no relation to a previous Arkansas State League that operated in 1908-1909) and it would be a Class D league under the supervision of the NAPBL.

Frank Mathews had the "temporary" removed from his title as president of the league and A.C. Beck of Bentonville was named vice-president. Clifford Shaw, Fayetteville; G.C. Killebrew, Siloam Springs; J.O. Clark, Rogers; and Tom McGill, Bentonville were named to the Board of Directors. Fred Hawn was named Fayetteville manager and the league decided upon an 87 game split-season, scheduled to start May 8. There were to be four games a week with double-headers on Sunday afternoons; the league would wind up play on Labor Day.

Enthusiasm for the league ran high and in addition to Fred Hawn at Fayetteville and "Red" Wilson in Bentonville, veteran baseball men Pete Casey and Clyde Glass were named managers at Rogers and Siloam Springs. Only one problem remained locally: getting Fayetteville a park to play in.

Negotiations were underway to use the Washington County Fair Grounds field but there was a snag that held the agreement up until the town of Harrison suggested on April 11 that they'd be happy to replace Fayetteville in the new league. Two days after that story hit the paper, Fayetteville found common ground with the Fair Grounds committee (for 10 percent of the gate receipts during the season) and Fayetteville's last obstacle to having a professional baseball team had been overcome.

"Arkansas State Loop Is 'All Set'" the *Daily Democrat* pronounced on April 18 and preseason training began right away. Each town in the league held baseball "schools," with as many as 50 players trying out, to refine and select their talent.

Teams would be pared down to fourteen players at the start of the season and then to twelve after ten additional days of league play. Each team could carry two "class" men, that is, players with prior professional experience. The remaining players would be classified as rookies: everyday players with less than ten games played as a pro; pitchers with no more than 54 innings of professional experience.

As the league moved towards its May 8 opening day then, Fayetteville had only one task left: finding a name for its new ball team. Most fans who remember or knew about Fayetteville's team in these old minor league days knew them as the Angels, but that's not the name they started with. Not at all. Fayetteville's first professional baseball team was going to be christened by the fans and they came up with a rather interesting choice.

The *Fayetteville Daily Democrat* decided to run a contest and let the locals name the team. "For the past two years," the paper advised, "a semi-pro team has been known here as the 'All-Stars' but that name won't do and it would be wise for entries not to pick it."

And so, while the unnamed team went through spring drills with players like Farmington's Buster Dunlap, University of Arkansas student Monroe "Monty" Johnson, local semi-pro stars Russell "Lefty" Poole and Homer "Doc" Ledbetter, David Bush of Chattanooga, Tennessee, "Woody" Salmons of Climax Springs, Missouri and Fayetteville boys Parker Rushing and Cline Watson trying out for a spot on the club, entries poured into the *Daily Democrat*'s name contest.

The "no-name" ball club, meanwhile, played two exhibition games late in April—losing a close contest to Rogers but then handily defeating Springdale's semi-pro town team 22-0—and the contest entries kept coming in. Finally on Tuesday, May 1, the contest closed. Judges Karl Greenhaw, Van Howell, and Marc Stice read the nearly 100 entries and there was a tie.

Two Fayetteville men, Louis M. Heerwagen and Raymond Mhoon, each received a free 44-game home season pass for coming up with a name highlighting one of Fayetteville's "outstanding advantages," its academic reputation. The name the fans chose: the Educators. The *Educators,* a sports fan might ask? It was hardly a name to strike terror into the hearts of roughneck opponents.

But Educators it was—soon shortened to the "Eds" by resourceful local sportswriters—and it was time to play ball. The rest of the league was set and they had some interesting names as well. Siloam Springs were the Buffaloes—a solid run-over-your-opponents name—but Bentonville and Rogers (at least at the beginning of the season) had names

Fayetteville in the 1930s
Photo courtesy of University of Arkansas Digital Collection #1652

hardly more fear-inspiring than the Educators. They were the Bentonville Officeholders and the Rogers Apple Knockers (rustics or hicks).

With colorful names like these, and with the natural rivalries existing among the cities in the league, the Arkansas State League was set. After several months of hard work and planning and with no shortage of obstacles that had been overcome, professional baseball was finally on in the Ozarks.

TWO
1934: The Educators

TUESDAY, MAY 8, 1934, was Opening Day—the first professional baseball game ever played in Fayetteville. The hometown Educators would be hosting the Siloam Springs Buffaloes in a 3 p.m. game at the Fair Grounds out "west of town on the Farmington-Prairie Grove-Westville highway." On Monday before the big first game, the *Daily Democrat* ran a full-page advertisement celebrating the first game and detailing prizes that Educators players could win from supportive local merchants.

Fayetteville Educators, 1934
Photo courtesy of Mrs. Russell Poole & A.D. Poole

The player with the first hit, for example, would receive a free car wash at H. L. Tuck Super Service. The first triple would get a player ten gallons of free gas from Heerwagen Bros. and the first player to walk could claim five free games of pool from the American Legion D.A.V. snooker parlor.

In the dubious reward category, Castle Luncheonette—which referred to itself as "Exclusive but not Expensive"—would give one dozen of the "World's Best Hamburgers" to the Educator committing the season's first error.

The town was primed and ready, the ballpark was secured and in fair shape, Umpire Tom Lunsford was scheduled to call 'em as he saw 'em, and the respective managers, seasoned baseball men Fred Hawn of Fayetteville and Clyde Glass of Siloam Springs, presented their opening day lineups.

Fayetteville Educators[7]	**Siloam Springs Buffaloes**
Les Wilson, CF	Kenneth Allum, SS
Cline Watson, RF	Russ Mosier, 3B
Monroe "Monty" Johnson, 2B	Ed Shaffer, 2B
Homer "Doc" Ledbetter, LF	Clyde Glass, CF
Parker Rushing, 1B	Flake, 1B
Allan Thomas, 3B	Moore, RF
Freddie Hawn, C	Douglas Scott, LF
Dave Bush, SS	Hines, C[8]
Russell Poole, P	Columbus "Chief" (Dry) Shell, P

For the ticket price of 25¢ for adults and 10¢ for kids, baseball fans now could watch a real live, honest to goodness minor league baseball game in Fayetteville, Arkansas.

Almost 350 fans (the Fair Grounds would seat up to 2,000) watched a high scoring, extra inning game with Siloam Springs defeating the hometown Educators in their first ever contest 9-7 in twelve innings. The game took three hours and fifteen minutes to complete and was umpired by a man named Craig, not the Tom Lunsford as had been advertised.

Up north on their home field, Bentonville defeated Rogers 12-7 in the other inaugural Arkansas State League game, as Mayor Sam Beasley threw out the first ball to his Rogers counterpart Mayor Ernest Vinson. With an official set of games completed, the Arkansas State League was on its way.

Despite losing the first professional game in Fayetteville, members of the Educators did score some of the prizes offered by Fayetteville merchants. With the team's first hit of the season, Parker Rushing got a free H.L. Tuck Super Service car wash. Herman Boshears hit a pinch-hit triple to take ten gallons of Heerwagen Brothers gas; and for committing the first error in Fayetteville professional baseball history, Cline Watson was awarded a dozen free hamburgers from the Castle Luncheonette.

In the first weeks of the brand new league and season the Educators played well enough, with Doc Ledbetter leading all hitters and Thornton "Hornbuckle Buck" Buchanan gaining three straight pitching victories.[9] Then, on May 17, not ten days into the season, the first of several changes that would affect the Educators' team chemistry occurred. Les Wilson, the Educators starting centerfielder, asked for his release from the club in order to take a better job with the Charleroi Tigers of the Class D Pennsylvania State Association.

That same afternoon Fayetteville beat the Rogers Apple Knockers behind Buchanan's pitching and Cline Watson's hitting. The very next day Rogers, apparently already tired of their fruity appellation, voted to rename themselves the Rustlers.

On May 23, *Daily Democrat* headlines carried the news that Bonnie Parker and Clyde Barrow had been shot dead in a hail of bullets down in Louisiana. The paper also revealed that when the outlaw couple died they were driving a car with a Fayetteville license plate reported stolen in April from the automobile of County Clerk Merle Cruse.[10]

Losing a shootout of their own the day before, the Educators were beaten by Bentonville and just days later (May 28) the Educators were in last place in the league. To top off the rapid fall, the league's

Russell Poole, 1934
Photo courtesy of Mrs. Russell Poole & A. D. Poole

leading hitter—Doc Ledbetter—left for Charleroi, too. Ledbetter had a remarkable .567 batting average when he got the call to move up.

As for the Educators, after Dave Bush and Russell Poole were ejected from a loss to Siloam Springs on May 29, a game in which Fayetteville finished a man short in the field, the team went on a five-game winning streak to move into a virtual tie for first on June 6.

The Educators stayed in first place, through the middle of the month. They beat Bentonville on June 8 and managed a double-header split with Siloam Springs on June 10. They followed that with wins over Bentonville on June 12 and 14 to reach first place. For local fans, the *Daily Democrat* standings for June 15 looked fine indeed.

Arkansas State League

Team	Won	Lost	Pct.
Fayetteville	15	12	.556
Siloam Springs	14	13	.519
Rogers	14	13	.519
Bentonville	11	16	.407

On June 15, Bentonville's ace pitcher Herb Wollard, whose twin brother Maurice was his catcher, pitched a seven-inning, 7-1 no-hitter—the first in league history—against the Rogers Rustlers, who scored their only run on an error. Wollard then beat the Educators 2-0, and the loss began a decline in Fayetteville's fortunes.

Mainstays Allan Thomas and Russell Poole left the club for regular jobs. Fred Hawn added outfielder Art Chestnut, ex-University of Arkansas star Charlie Crawford, and pitcher Al Robello, of Livermore, California—as well as a high school friend of heavyweight champion Max Baer. The new players helped give the Educators some wins, but the team continued to tail off.

On June 17, when Thomas and Poole left the team, the Educators split a pair of contests with Bentonville, then lost two games to Rogers (one to Rustlers ace pitcher and future New York Yankee Marvin Breuer). Fayetteville won their next game but then dropped four consecutive decisions to Rogers and Bentonville, which was led by hard-hitting Harold Ensley, later known to many TV fans as "The Sportsman's Friend."[11]

Staggering towards the first-half finish, the Educators ended up losing eleven of their last fourteen games. Bentonville on the other hand, now managed by Morris "Cy" Young, who replaced "Red" Wilson in mid-June, leapfrogged Fayetteville into third place by winning eleven of their last eighteen. Siloam Springs defeated Rogers twice on the last day of the first half to tie the Rustlers for first place.

Arkansas State League
(Final standings—first half)

Team	Won	Lost	Pct.
Rogers	24	21	.533
Siloam Springs	24	21	.533
Bentonville	22	23	.489
Fayetteville	20	25	.444

One of the good things about a split-season format is that all teams start again at square one for the second half. Even though Siloam Springs and Rogers still had to play a one-game playoff to decide the first half winner and then that winner had to take on a team of All-Stars to give the fans an extra treat, regular league play started right back up.

With only a day off, the Educators met Siloam Springs July 10 at the Fair Grounds and, in front of the smallest crowd of the year, lost 11-3. The *Daily Democrat* expressed manager Fred Hawn's "desperate" need to get new life into his struggling club and called for fans to support the team, especially when they started winning again. Improbable as it seemed at that moment, that's just what the Educators did.

They won seven of their next nine games and by late July were in first place, one-half game ahead of Bentonville. Along the way, the Educators beat Siloam Springs three straight times. On July 16, Rogers won the one-game playoff 5-2 at Siloam Springs to capture the first-half pennant, as Rogers pitcher J.W. White held the Buffaloes hitless until the ninth inning.

Back in regular season play, Rogers beat Fayetteville 13-2 but then the Educators reeled off four straight wins over the Rustlers to reach first place. During this stretch, Les Wilson—back from a brief stint in the Pennsylvania State Association—and Cline Watson each asked for his release from the team after Fred Hawn had brought in new players Virgil Norton, Randall Garns, and Stubby Carnes. Despite all the comings and goings, on July 24 the Educators still stood atop the second-half heap.

Unfortunately, the Educators soon began to falter. After the league All-Stars (overloaded with team manager Fred Hawn's Fayetteville players) beat first-half pennant winners Rogers 8-6 on July 23, the Educators started a skid that would see them lose fourteen of their last twenty games. But they weren't alone in their collapse.

The previously powerful Siloam Springs Buffaloes, demoralized by a league ruling that caused them to forfeit four wins over Bentonville (later amended to two) for using too many "class men"—that is, players with previous minor league experience—fell from the top of the league to also-rans.

Attendance in both cities suffered and the two franchises struggled to stay afloat. Fred Hawn had taken over Cliff Shaw's interest in Fayetteville towards the end of the first half-season and was now "in full control of the Educators destinies."

Hawn did his best, but with low attendance, a field that was best described as "rough," and a struggling team, times were hard. It showed on the field.

From first place on July 24, the Educators began to drop like a stone. They lost five in a row to Bentonville with only 150 fans showing up at the Fair Grounds for the first of those games. After the Educators lost their sixth decision in a row at the hands of Siloam Springs on July 31, something had to give. It was Fred Hawn.

On August 1 the *Daily Democrat* reported that Hawn had given up the Fayetteville franchise to league president Frank Matthews of Rogers. In order to take over the Fayetteville club, Mathews stepped down from the presidency (Charles "Chuck" Morgan of Joplin, Missouri replaced him) and with some help from local merchants raised the $225 needed to pay past due salaries and bills.

Mathews was a non-playing manager, and after a couple of days off, Hawn returned to his regular catching duties with the club. Several local fans present at the Chamber of Commerce where the franchise switch took place expressed their concern and uncertainty as to why Fayetteville, the league's largest city, had not been supporting their team.

The league did get one boost that day, however, as Johnny Nee, a scout for the New York Yankees, sent the *Daily Democrat* a special report from Durham, North Carolina. Baseball needs leagues like the Arkansas State, Nee said, to get young players started off in professional ball. Times may be rough, especially in a "new enterprise" like this, he opined, but things "will be much easier next season" and "the loop will be a first-class cradle of baseball."

Thanks also to the forfeit ruling whereby Siloam Springs and Bentonville each ended up losing two of the games in their "class men" protest, the Fayetteville club, even after losing six in a row, was still in the second-half race as a result of a 14-11 win over Siloam Springs August 1 at the Fair Grounds. The victory ended the Educators losing streak on the day Frank Mathews debuted as their manager.

Thornton Buchanan, 1934
Photo courtesy of Mrs. Russell Poole & A. D. Poole

Cline Watson then came back from a brief defection to Bentonville and the Educators added the league's most traded player, Douglas Scott—from Rogers, by way of Siloam Springs—to its roster. More player changes came on August 3 when Harold Ensley came over from Bentonville and Mack Bolding, a right-handed pitcher, arrived from the Western Association.

With "Hornbuckle Buck" Buchanan pitching a win over Siloam Springs on August 3, a game in which the big lefthander also batted in the winning run, Fayetteville's Educators took two of their next three games (they also beat Siloam Springs on "Mothers Appreciation Day") to fight their way back to second place by August 6. But they then lost five games in a row, including a double-header to Siloam Springs on August 12, and fell unceremoniously into dead last place.

On Tuesday, August 14, the *Daily Democrat* reported a real shocker of a deal as the Educators traded All-Star shortstop Dave Bush to Rogers for the standard "player to be named later" (a subsequent rumor said the deal was a straight cash transaction of $50). Woodrow Bussy, a Vinita, Oklahoma shortstop was signed to replace Bush. The Educators promptly lost again to Bentonville (their eleventh straight loss to the Officeholders) before finally beating the same club on August 15 to end the losing skid.

On August 16 only 61 fans turned out at the Fair Grounds to watch the Educators beat Bentonville a second straight time and when they lost at Bentonville on August 17, rumors of the league folding early were rampant. Siloam Springs was not getting good crowds either and as early as August 14 were said to be on the verge of dropping out of the league. Springdale, Arkansas and Cassville and Seligman in Missouri had been suggested as being willing to take Siloam Springs' place but, as was later learned, league officials had already met and decided to close the season early.

Despite the rumors and behind the scenes goings on, Fayetteville played on, in fact winning a final game over Bentonville at the Fair Grounds on Sunday, August 19. That same day Siloam Springs decided "to call it a season" and Fayetteville was "glad to call it quits" with them.[12]

Robert Henry, president of the Siloam Springs club, cleared the rumor air with a letter to the *Fort Smith Southwest-Times Record* (whose sports reporter Johnnie Porter covered the Arkansas State League) reprinted in the *Fayetteville Daily Democrat* on August 20.

Parker Rushing, 1934
Photo courtesy of Mrs. Russell Poole & A. D. Poole

"On Monday night Aug. 13," the letter read in part, "there was called a meeting of the league... It was agreed upon that we would close the season Aug. 15, and the play-off would start Sunday, Aug. 19 between Rogers and Bentonville." Mr. Henry added in his letter that the season was closed "on account of the dry, hot weather that cut our attendance until it would not pay to play."

He went on to assure everyone that the ballplayers had been paid in full and that Siloam Springs would definitely keep their team for the next season. Siloam Springs had gotten permission from Judge Bramham and the NAPBL to close the season, Mr. Henry stated, as long as they (Siloam Springs) paid all the players and all the club's bills. Since they had done all this, he noted, it was hoped that this matter had been "straightened out with regard to Siloam Springs' interest in the league."

And so, just like that, the inaugural season of the Arkansas State League came to an abrupt end. Had the season gone its full 87 games as originally planned, perhaps the Educators could have found a way out of the league cellar, but as it was they ended up last in the league in both halves of the split season.

Calling off the rest of the year's games was probably a blessing, however, not only for the team but also for those who had to watch them as well. Not only were the Educators ready to fold, but as the *Daily Democrat* reported after the last game: "Fayetteville's uniforms also were ready to close the season. There isn't a whole suit in the bunch and the cloth contains more dirt than cloth."

The final standings for the second half of the 1934 season looked like this:

Arkansas State League
(Final standings—second half)

Team	Won	Lost	Pct.
Bentonville	18	12	.600
Siloam Springs	13	13	.500
Rogers	12	14	.462
Fayetteville	13	17	.433

The league championship was a spirited best of seven series between first-half champions Rogers and second-half winners Bentonville, which was leading the league when it shut down the second half-season early. The first six contests, featuring some good pitching by both clubs, were split three games apiece. Rogers captured the league championship September 3 with a 7-0 victory before 1,000 fans who "braved cold weather" to watch the final game in Rogers.

Rocky as the road had been, the Arkansas State League managed to survive its first year of existence. There had been some good ball played in the league and several players, such as Bentonville's Bill Beams and Herb Wollard; Rogers' Bill Homan and Marvin Breuer; Siloam Springs' Clyde Glass and Cotton Hill; and Fayetteville's Parker Rushing, Fred Hawn, and Al Robello had emerged as stars.

Fayetteville's Educators hadn't done particularly well either as a team or as a franchise in their initial season, but they had had their moments. At the very least, professional baseball had been established in town and Fayetteville's boosters could look forward to 1935 with the hope that things would pick up for the local team. As die-hard fans always say of their losing teams, "there's always next year."

THREE
1935: The Bears

THE OFF-SEASON between 1934 and 1935, marked by the violent deaths of more of the era's famous gun-wielding outlaws including Pretty Boy Floyd and Baby Face Nelson, saw continued change and rumor of change for the Arkansas State League. The *Fayetteville Daily Democrat* speculated that neither Pete Casey, manager of the 1934 Rogers Rustlers, nor Clyde Glass, his counterpart at Siloam Springs, was expected to guide those same teams in 1935.

There was also the ongoing concern about Fayetteville's ability to support its hometown team because their ballpark, located on the far west side of town, was "too far from the business sector." League umpiring would be improved, it was hoped, because new candidates were being trained at Ray Doan's school for umpires in Hot Springs. In addition, the paper reported, league president Chuck Morgan and other club officials were discussing the idea of enlarging the league to six clubs for 1935.

As early as fall 1934, the *Daily Democrat* reported a potentially big change for the financially struggling baseball franchises of the fledgling league. The first year economic tribulations of the Fayetteville, Siloam Springs, Bentonville, and Rogers clubs might be alleviated by some fiscal backing from "on high." On high referring to possible economic support coming to the little class D league all the way from the heights of Major League baseball itself.

Al G. Eckert, president of the Springfield, Missouri, Class C team in the St. Louis Cardinals farm system, after touring the cities in the Arkansas State League in the first week of November, told local officials that St. Louis most likely "would be willing" to take control of the entire league. The proposition would have Springfield, through its parent organization, giving financial aid to the Arkansas State League and overseeing its operation, including furnishing players for teams in order to develop them for St. Louis.

In January 1935, Arkansas State League officials met in Rogers and re-elected Chuck Morgan as the circuit's president. Morgan and the heads of the clubs—J. O. Clark of Rogers, Frank Mathews of Fayetteville (by way of Rogers), Arlie Beck of Bentonville and Robert Henry of Siloam Springs—met with representatives of towns looking to join the league. Springdale, Berryville, and Harrison in Arkansas and Tahlequah, Oklahoma, sent officials to the meeting and people from Monett and Cassville, Missouri, were expected but ended up not attending.

Ray "Rabbit" Powell
Photo courtesy of Library of Congress

Only a few days later, Judge Kennesaw Mountain Landis, hard-nosed commissioner of major league baseball, made an ominous ruling that after 1935 "no club will be permitted to have a working agreement with an entire league, or with more than one club in a league."

Although Judge Landis, who considered the Cardinals farm system "intolerable and un-American,"[13] would eventually have a serious contention with St. Louis over this ruling, the agreement between the Cardinals and the Arkansas State League had been made prior to the judge's ruling and would not affect the league in 1935.

Meanwhile, preparations for the new season moved ahead. In late February, Bentonville and Siloam Springs hired two veteran baseball men, Wilbur "Cordwood" Davis and Ray Powell, respectively, as their managers for the upcoming campaign. Powell had been a big leaguer years before, playing centerfield for the Boston Braves on May 1, 1920 in what, at the time, was the longest major league game in history, a 26-inning marathon 1-1 tie between the Braves and the Brooklyn Dodgers.[14]

Cordwood Davis had only made the proverbial "cup of coffee" stop in the majors, but in 1924, while at Okmulgee in the Class C Western Association, he had an extraordinary season, batting .400, driving in 190 runs, and hitting 51 home runs. The only reason Cordwood did not win the league triple crown outright was that teammate Cecil "Stormy" Davis, no relation, also hit 51 home runs that year.[15]

As the 1935 regular season neared, Fayetteville's franchise, still in the hands of Rogers' Frank Mathews, hung in the balance. It was estimated that $3000 would be needed to get the club through the season. Gate receipts were expected to be around $1800 for the season, and the St. Louis Cardinals arrangement would bring the team an additional $200 a month. If local merchants and businessmen could raise between $150-$200 more per month, the club would probably be able to survive.

In March, Fayetteville businessmen did what many in the city and league had hoped they would, they bought the franchise from Mathews for a reported $75 and the $250 needed to join the NAPBL. New board members for the club were designated and included: Marc Stice, chairman; Bernal Seamster, secretary and treasurer; W. C. "Pete" Morton, Herman Tuck and Monroe Laner.

Rogers had been the only team in the league to make money in 1934 and Fayetteville officials knew that to emulate the Rustlers they would have to improve last year's home paid attendance at the Fair Grounds (estimated at 8,000). They hoped to draw 10-15,000 fans this year and they were well aware that they would need "cooperation, and lots of it" from local fans do so.

Still, when Fayetteville signed Pete Casey, manager of the 1934 league champions from Rogers, and then learned that radio station KUOA would likely broadcast some of the club's games, chips for the

1935 season looked like they were falling in place.

With manager Casey ready to start the annual spring baseball "school" for player hopefuls on April 15, Fayetteville found itself in the same place it had been the year before, looking for a new team name. The first year nickname, Educators, was deemed "out" for the upcoming season and fans were asked to submit entries once again. While Fayetteville fans were deciding what to call their club, Rogers hired Fred Cato, an old teammate of Fayetteville's Pete Casey at Okmulgee in the Western Association, as their new manager.

"Add Two Clubs to State League," 1935 *Fayetteville Daily Democrat*

On April 8, the league announced the 1935 season would begin May 9. The first half season would end July 7, the second half September 2. Two umpires, Les Wilson—who had played for the Educators in 1934 but also did some umpiring late in the season—and one-armed Jack Clemmens were signed for the year. The next day, Fayetteville announced it would have a "knothole gang" for kids under 12—allowing youngsters free admission to all regular weekday games and with only a 5¢ charge on Sundays and holidays.

Kenneth Brooks of 231 Mill Street won the contest to rename the Fayetteville club. The team would not be known as the "Prohibitionists" as one wag suggested, referring to the legal absence of liquor stores in town, but instead would carry the less political and more powerful nickname: "Bears." Brooks was awarded a season pass for his winning entry.

April 15, opening day of Pete Casey's baseball school, found 50 ballplayers (a total of 78 would eventually report) vying for spots on the Fayetteville club. There were a number of familiar faces among those trying out including Jake Drake, Allan Thomas, Paul Linch, and Parker Rushing from the 1934 squad. Then with less than a week before spring practice, the league announced it was expanding to six teams.

Huntsville, from over in Madison County, would be joining the league, as would a team from Cassville, Missouri, the first league franchise from out of state. It was shortly reported that young Jim Nicely (only 24) would pilot Huntsville, while Ed Hawks, who had managed Rogers and Bentonville in 1934, would guide the new Cassville entry.

By the first week of May, the 1935 exhibition season, troubled by frequent washouts, was in as full a swing as it would get. The Bears split their first two scrimmage games with Rogers, then won a final pre-season contest on May 7 against Siloam Springs at the Fair Grounds. Offering 50 game packages for $7.50, a savings of $5.00 over purchasing individual tickets at 25¢ each, and with the team sporting their new "dark grey and red" uniforms, the Bears were ready for the season opener on the road at Cassville.

Around the league, the talk was mostly about ballparks. Siloam Springs had a new field—Smiley Park; Bentonville's slugging manager, Cordwood Davis, took a good look at his park's short right field fence and decided to "leave her like it was;" and Huntsville chose to go with their short left-field fence as well, unless "too many flies sail over (it) for home runs." Cassville, it was determined by those who had seen it, would have "the best park in the league."

Rogers' main concern was not their park but their name. They didn't want to be the Rustlers anymore, so they initiated a contest, much like Fayetteville had done, to come up with a new nickname. They settled, appropriately enough in a league sponsored by St. Louis, on calling themselves the Cardinals.

Siloam Springs didn't want to be the Buffaloes anymore, either, so they renamed themselves the Travelers. The two new clubs, Cassville and Huntsville, were called the Tigers and the Red Birds, respectively. Only Bentonville started out with their 1934 name—the Officeholders—but late in the 1935 season they would change, too, to the White Sox.

With spring training completed and the team names mostly settled, the Arkansas State League was ready to open action as a six team, two-state entity. There would be two sets of opening days. May 9, Fayetteville would play at Cassville, Bentonville at Rogers, and Siloam Springs at Huntsville. The following day the same teams would play each other at the other club's park for a second day of home openers.

Fayetteville was planning to have a big day for their first game at the Fair Grounds. Recently elected Mayor, A.D. McAllister would be there to throw out the first ball and the Fayetteville High School band would play between innings. Special areas of the grandstand were to be reserved for the Knothole Gang and—as was the reality of the time—the paper noted that a "section of the stand (sic) for colored fans also has been set aside."

Before the Bears could have their home opener against Ed Hawks' Cassville team, however, they had to travel to Missouri on May 9 to take on the Tigers at their ballpark. Six hundred "baseball-crazy Missourians" braved the elements—there was a pre-game downpour and then intermittent rain the rest of the day, turning the field into a swamp—to watch the local heroes beat the visiting Arkansans in a game "featuring" 14 errors, 7 by each team. In the other two league openers, Rogers beat Bentonville at home while Siloam Springs lost at Huntsville.

Next day, despite threatening weather, 650 Fayetteville fans watched the Bears return the favor by beating Cassville at the Fair Grounds. Southpaw Paul Linch threw a six-hitter at the Tigers—all decked out in their new black and gold uniforms—and struck out nine to take the opening day victory.

Fayetteville's starting lineup was as follows:

Allan Thomas	CF
Monty Johnson	2B
Doug White	3B
Parker Rushing	1B
Paul Rucker	C
Charlie Johnson	SS
Henry Maus	RF
Gerald Tobey	LF
Paul Linch	P

As advertised, the game was broadcast on KUOA with David Byrn calling the action. Up in Siloam Springs, Huntsville defeated the renamed Travelers for the second straight day. The Rogers at Bentonville tilt was rained out.

Just like opening day in 1934, local merchants awarded special prizes for Fayetteville season firsts. Paul Rucker won a free car wash from Tuck's Super Service and a dozen cans of peaches from Ozark Grocery for getting the Bear's first hit and first run in the home opener. Henry Maus took home three-pound cans of coffee from both Fayetteville Mercantile and Griffin Grocery for getting the first walk and scoring the winning run. Fortunately, no one this year, offered a prize for the team's first error.

With the regular season underway, the Bears and the rest of the league found their toughest opponent to be the weather. There were numerous rainouts and many games were shortened or affected by the rain. After a week and a half of play, during which time the league members agreed to carry 14 players and a manager (playing or not) on each team, newcomer Huntsville was in first place by percentage points over Rogers.

On Saturday, May 18, Monty Johnson and Parker Rushing led the Bears to a win over Cassville on the Tigers' home field. Even at this early date in the season a couple of changes had already occurred on the team and in the league. Peter Negri, left-handed outfielder from Zeigler, Illinois, joined the Bears replacing opening day star Henry

ANGELS IN THE OZARKS

Season Opening Day Ad, May 1935
Fayetteville Daily Democrat

Maus, and Les Wilson of last year's Fayetteville team was officially signed by the league as an umpire—actually calling the Bears' win at Cassville.

Through much of May, the Bears played yo-yo ball, up one day and down the next. Rogers, on the other hand, used a six-game winning streak to hold onto the league lead until Cassville ran off eight straight wins of its own to sit atop the standings on May 29. Bentonville lost seven of eight games to fall into sole possession of last place with Siloam Springs nipping at their retreating heels.

If you had had 2¢ on June 1, the price of a copy of the *Fayetteville Daily Democrat*, you would have read that the Bears split a double-header with Bentonville and you would have seen that currently injured Bears second baseman, Monty Johnson, was leading the league with a robust .484 batting average.

You also would have learned that day that the Bears had added more new players, including outfielders John Evans and Max Sharum and pitcher Bob Springer. It was additionally reported that KUOA, newly purchased by John Brown University, was going to discontinue broadcasting Bears games from the Fair Grounds. It was a rather busy day for Bear reporting.

By June 3, when Siloam Springs won their ninth straight game by beating Fayetteville, the Travelers had reversed their recent run of bad fortune and had climbed to third place in league standings. In the first game of a double-header the following day, new Bear pitcher Warren "Moose" Fralich halted the Travelers streak with a 16-4 Fayetteville win.

In between rainouts (9 inches of rain fell on June 6 in only 15 hours time in nearby Vinita, Oklahoma) the Bears were beaten twice by the Rogers Cardinals who were playing so well they threatened to leave the rest of the league behind.

The Rogers hitting attack was led by Tom Cooper, who hit home runs of epic proportions off Bears (and everyone else's) pitching. The Rogers catcher, playing under his more familiar first name of Walker, would go on to have an outstanding major league career during which, in the early and mid-1940s, he teamed with his brother Mort to give the St. Louis Cardinals one of the finest pitcher-catcher combinations of the era.

On June 11, the same day that the city passed a long awaited and debated law allowing for the legal sale of liquor by retailers and wholesalers, the Bears were beaten soundly by Siloam Springs. The Democrat groaned that "another miserable account of themselves before the home folks was chalked up by the Fayetteville Bears at the Fair Grounds." With the season only a month old, things were not looking good for the Bears.

While Rogers continued to be the best team by far, attendance around the league was not what officials had hoped for. Siloam Springs—like Fayetteville not doing much to impress its fans—began to play a few "home" games in Monett, Missouri. Fayetteville and Cassville also played a game at Monett in June ("wet-water" springs had made Cassville's "best park in the league" unusable) and the league even gave Rogers permission to move to Monett if they wanted to—which they didn't.

Meanwhile, the Bears, behind the fine pitching of Moose Fralich, managed to beat the Huntsville Red Birds with Les Wilson, 1934 Fayetteville player and current league umpire, joining the team to replace catcher Paul Rucker who was out of town. Also missing from the Bears was manager Pete Casey, who was recovering from mild sunstroke.

By June 17, the Bears had added more new players including Pete Ashmore, an infielder, and Lawson Rinckey, a pitcher. The additions didn't help much as Ed Hawks brought his Cassville Tigers, the "surprise" team of the league, to town on June 18 and defeated the Bears twice at the Fair Grounds (second games of league doubleheaders were usually only seven-innings long). After losing to Rogers the following day, Fayetteville found itself alone at the bottom of the league standings.

In the next week, change continued to be the byword for both the Bears and the rest of the league. While Rogers beat the Bears for the ninth time in nine tries, former Fayetteville player "Hornbuckle Buck" Buchanan threw an artful three-hit shutout for Cassville over Bentonville (both games played June 20).

Huntsville's manager Jim Nicely was let go, even on the day when the fine young first baseman was the middle man in a rare triple play.[16] The Bears made more player moves by releasing pitchers Dempsey Alexander and Fred Springer as well as infielders Charlie Johnson and Gordy Oster and then signed John Rogers, an outfielder, and pitcher Carl Jensen.

On "Bloody Sunday," June 23 (when four players from each team, including Fayetteville's Paul Rucker, Doug White, Moose Fralich and Monty Johnson were all injured), the Bears beat Huntsville twice to climb out of the league cellar. The next day, Cassville had to forfeit five games (later amended to four) for using an ineligible player and the Tigers' first half pennant hopes were all but dashed. On June 27, Rogers surprised everyone by releasing manager Fred Cato in an economic "retrenchment" move, even though the club was now solidly in first place.

That same day, the Bears knocked out six homers, including two by Doug White, who had split his finger during Bloody Sunday's battle, to defeat Cassville on the Missourians home field. Despite that win, and on the same day that Jim Nicely's departure from Huntsville was printed, June 29, the *Daily Democrat* also reported that Fayetteville manager, Pete Casey, had been released and immediately replaced by the recently fired skipper of the first place Rogers Cardinals, Fred Cato.

Under Cato, the Bears made a last ditch effort to get into the first half pennant race. On the new manager's first day at the helm, July 1, they swept two from Cassville at the Fair Grounds. The next day they repeated the sweep, this time in Cassville. With solid hitting from Pete Ashmore, Les Wilson, and Dick Murray (at first base now for the departed Parker Rushing) and with complete game victories from pitchers Moose Fralich, Ike Rorie, Lawson Rinckey and Paul Linch, the Bears seemed revitalized.

They followed with a fifth straight win under Cato, their sixth in a row overall, beating Huntsville on July 3 to move into fourth place in the league. A Fourth of July loss to Siloam Springs, who were all decked out in their new "flaming red" uniforms, however, ended the Bears hot streak in front of 800 faithful at the Fair Grounds and closed out the first half of the season. A proposed game between Rogers and a squad of league All-Stars was called off due to injuries to Cardinals players.

Injuries notwithstanding, Rogers held on to win the first half season pennant just as they had in 1934, while Siloam Springs, winning

14 of their last 22, had vaulted over the sliding Cassville Tigers into second place. Despite their own late run, the Bears settled for fourth ahead of Huntsville and Bentonville.

Arkansas State League
(Final standings—first half)

Team	Won	Lost	Pct.
Rogers	33	21	.611
Siloam Springs	30	24	.556
Cassville	25	22	.532
Fayetteville	21	25	.457
Huntsville	21	28	.429
Bentonville	21	31	.404

When the second half of the Arkansas State League season opened, there was ominous international news of an imminent Italian invasion of Ethiopia. On the national scene, famed G-man Melvin Purvis suddenly quit his high profile crime-stopper job, and locally the weather service reported there had been nearly 40 inches of rain during the last six months, including 13.06 inches in June. The wettest day was June 17 when 2.84 inches of rain had fallen.

Around Arkansas State League ballparks, things picked up about where they'd left off. The Fayetteville Bears won a couple, then lost a couple. Rogers, as might be expected, won all of their games at the start and didn't lose until the Bears knocked them off in a 1-0 pitcher's duel July 12 at the Fair Grounds.

That same day Johnny John of Cassville equaled the old nine-inning league record when he struck out 15 Siloam Springs Travelers, but Bentonville's Albert White did John one better by fanning 16 Huntsville batters, also that day, to immediately establish a new record. For good measure Fayetteville beat Huntsville in 13 innings the following day as the Bears' Jim Jensen struck out 18 Red Birds in the eleven innings he worked. All in all, it was a couple of great days for power pitchers.

After consecutive low scoring, extra-inning games, the Bears lost to Bentonville 13-10 before 700 at the Fair Grounds on July 14, then went to Bentonville the next day and beat the Officeholders 12-11. When the dust cleared, the Bears were tied for second place, with Siloam Springs one game back of Rogers. Three days later, July 18, after consecutive wins over Bentonville and Cassville, the Bears were actually atop the league in a dead heat with Rogers.

Hanging out at such rarefied heights proved to be too much for the Bears, however, and they quickly dropped two games, including a July 19 loss to Cassville's Johnny John, who the paper said "hails from a John Street in some city in Louisiana."

On the plus side, Bears second baseman, Monty Johnson, began tearing the cover off the ball. Johnson had ten multi-hit games in the team's next eleven contests. During the streak he also hit four home runs over a five-game stretch. Johnson's batting average for the remarkable eleven-game span was an astounding .612 (30 for 49).

Johnson's heroics helped the Bears tie Rogers for first again, but remarkably, by the end of the second baseman's streak—he went hitless in two straight Bears losses to Siloam Springs on July 25 and 26—Fayetteville had dropped to fourth place in the league. Meanwhile, Rogers' big-league-to-be catcher, Tom (Walker) Cooper, hit five home runs in four games to help his team keep Siloam Springs in second place.

In Fayetteville, the Bears continued to make personnel changes. Chicago city league pitcher Ed Bohne came on board and Allan Thomas got off to take an oil job in Wichita Falls, Texas. "Likeable" Ralph Radabaugh signed up to play centerfield and Les Wilson officially re-signed with the club to play third base.

Even former Fayetteville star player Doc Ledbetter reappeared, after playing for Bartlesville of the Western Association and Monessen of the Pennsylvania State Association. Concerns about where Ledbetter would play for the Bears were alleviated when the big slugger signed on with the Rogers Cardinals instead. Over in Huntsville, the Red Birds leading pitcher, ill-fated Charley Wilson, had taken the helm of the struggling Madison County team from Jim Nicely.

On July 24, the last day of Monty Johnson's hitting streak, a Merchant's Day[17] crowd of 1,000 fans saw Fayetteville move into undisputed possession of second place with a 12-5 punishing of Siloam Springs at the Fair Grounds.

Pete Ashmore, Bears shortstop, hit the longest home run of the season beyond the wire fence in left field and Moose Fralich, never a big home run threat, hit a grand slam—although it must be pointed out that the ball was actually lost in the deep, unmowed grass in right field. Walter J. Lemke of the *Daily Democrat* swore, tongue firmly in cheek as usual, that while Moose rounded the bases on his grand slam he "stopped at every base to look the situation over."[18]

After two losses to Siloam Springs, the Bears settled into the middle of the pack and stayed there awhile. Around the league, Walker Cooper had taken the batting lead with a .355 average and his teammate Cotton Hill had run off ten straight wins to pace all pitchers with a sparkling 11-1 record.

Moose Fralich, of the Bears, continued his mastery of the league leading Cardinals, shutting them out July 28 for the second consecutive time (Fralich pitched 22 straight scoreless innings in the extended hot streak) in front of 850 folks at the Fair Grounds. But when July ended, Rogers was still in first and the Bears were just a .500 club.

August opened with a couple of small flourishes. Bentonville ended a short five-game win streak that tightened up the middle four slots in the standings and Doc Ledbetter, new of Rogers, had six hits in six at bats, including a game winning triple, in the Cardinals' win over Cassville on August 1.

The Bears, never one to let moss grow over a dugout bench, released former University of Arkansas star Paul Rucker, as well as John Evans, the "likeable" Ralph Radabaugh and Dick Murray. Murray's slot was filled by the signing of "big" Hal Frederick, who was to be counted on for some extra base hitting.

The following night, one of the oddest tragic events ever connected with the Arkansas State League occurred. Barely more than twenty-four hours after driving in the winning run in a Huntsville victory over Siloam Springs, Red Birds manager Charley Wilson fell to his death from the top of the Ferris Wheel at a Huntsville carnival.

Over the weekend fans and players around the league stood for a moment of silent tribute to the fallen manager. The stunned Red Birds, now managed by catcher Bill Werner (who was with Wilson in the Ferris Wheel chair but was able to cling on to it and, thus, save his own life), somehow found a way to defeat Rogers on Sunday, August 4.[19]

In what surely must qualify as one of life's stranger ironies, league president Morgan made Huntsville forfeit the game they won the night before Wilson's death because the Red Birds had used three class men (players with previous minor league experience) in the game: Dan Kimball, Mack Bolding, and the late manager and pitcher, Charley Wilson himself.

As league play continued after the tragedy, the Fayetteville Bears lost three games in a row, including identical 8-3 losses to Siloam Springs and Cassville on consecutive days. But when Monty Johnson hit a dramatic tenth inning home run to beat Huntsville on August 7, the Bears were still in third place only four games behind new league leader, Siloam Springs. The Travelers had won six of seven to catch and pass Rogers.

On Sunday, August 11, the Bears had their best offensive day of the season, a 22-2 victory over league-leading Siloam Springs. The Bears' Moose Fralich won his twelfth game of the year to match the Travelers' Cotton Hill for most league wins while Monty Johnson had five hits and Allan Thomas (back from the Texas oil fields), Hal Frederick, and Manager Fred Cato had four hits apiece for Fayetteville. Siloam Springs won the next day behind the pitching of a fellow named Clint Raper whom the paper described as the "best losing pitcher" on the Travelers' roster.

The August 16 sports page of the *Daily Democrat* carried the news of a Bears victory over Rogers at the Fair Grounds, but one can imagine that few people made it so far into the paper that day as the front-page banner headline proclaimed *"Rogers And Post Killed in Plane Crash."*

Locals particularly mourned the loss of Rogers for he had strong northwest Arkansas ties, having married school teacher Betty Blake of the city of Rogers. The Oklahoma-born former cow puncher and famed humorist had also endeared himself to Fayetteville residents by working a benefit show to help save a tree-lined esplanade on an avenue near the University of Arkansas.

Back in Arkansas State League baseball, Siloam Springs continued to dominate, posting three straight wins over Fayetteville's Bears to take a solid four game lead over sliding Rogers. Duane (Dee) Kratzer of Cassville went on an extended hitting streak of 25 straight games from July 15 to August 13 to set a league record.

As the month wound down, Fayetteville continued its on-again off-again play. They seemed to do better on the road than at home, winning at Cassville on August 22, then losing to Cassville and Rogers at the Fair Grounds, the latter game attended by St. Louis Cardinals scouts, Joe Shultz and Eddie Dyer.

On the road again, the Bears beat Rogers in a benefit for the Arkansas Children's Home and Hospital and, as part of the league's arrangement with St. Louis, it was announced that Bears stars Monty Johnson and Moose Fralich had been chosen to move up a notch and finish the year with the Class C Springfield Cardinals of the Western Association.

As bad luck would have it, however, in the very next game, August 27, Johnson was hit in the head by a pitch in the first inning. Local favorite Fred Hawn, who had been brought back just days before to substitute catch for the injury-plagued Bears, played for the head-sore, but not seriously injured Johnson, and proceeded to field flawlessly and get two hits as well. Johnson took most of the remaining regular season off but it didn't seem to affect the team's play one way or another.

On August 28, the Bears dropped a 24-4 decision to Bentonville, a game in which the team "didn't take much interest after the Sox scored some runs and almost all players changed positions sometime during the tilt." In the game, Ace Villipique, Bentonville centerfielder, set a league record by stealing four bases in one inning.

This game seemed to be the first expression of what Walter Lemke said became a custom in the league: that was, turning "the last game of the season into a burlesque" (though this game was not the Bears last in 1935) if "the outcome wouldn't make any change in the final standings."[20]

The following day, Siloam Springs pitcher Clint Raper shut down Rogers to clinch the second half title for the Travelers. Fayetteville, on the other hand, continued to stumble, losing two of three games with Bentonville and ending the season September 2 with a loss to the Siloam Springs champions.

Only the weaker play of the hapless Huntsville Red Birds kept Fayetteville, losers of five of their last six games, from plummeting to the league cellar. The standings at the end of the season were:

Arkansas State League
(Final standings—second half)

Team	Won	Lost	Pct.
Siloam Springs	36	19	.655
Bentonville	30	25	.545
Cassville	29	26	.527
Rogers	26	29	.473
Fayetteville	24	31	.436
Huntsville	20	35	.364

In the league post-season playoffs, Siloam Springs opened with a home win over Rogers on September 4 in front of over 1,000 fans. Next day, 1,000 more watched Rogers square the series at 1-1 with a win at their park. Siloam Springs followed with a win at home in front of yet another 1,000-plus crowd when rightfielder, Jack Love, stole home for the game's only run.

Then, on September 9, "under threatening weather conditions," only about 500 fans were lucky enough to see Walker Cooper's "terrific bolt," a three-run home run, sail past the left field fence for an exciting 3-0, eleven-inning Rogers win. Despite a home run by Doc Ledbetter and Cooper's third of the series, Siloam Springs defeated Rogers the next day to take a commanding 3 games to 2 lead.

Rogers Cardinals, 1935
Photo courtesy of John G. Hall

Unfazed, Rogers beat Siloam Springs on the road, in a game marred by 10 errors, to tie the series again and force a decisive seventh game. Before 2500 fans on September 12, Rogers eked out a hard fought 6-5 win at home to repeat as league champions.

With a final flash of good pitching and hitting, the second season of the Arkansas State League—its last under that name—came to a fitting end.

FOUR
1936: The Arkansas-Missouri League

THE NEW YEAR'S Day edition of the *Fayetteville Daily Democrat* for January 1, 1936, featured a front-page photographic collage of the "Biggest Stories of 1935." Among these were the Italian invasion of Ethiopia, the Huey Long assassination, the trial and conviction of accused Lindbergh baby kidnapper Bruno Richard Hauptmann, and the airplane crash deaths of Wiley Post and Will Rogers.

Despite the generally gloomy tone of those headlines, this was also the first day of a new year and there was a feeling of optimism that the U.S. economy would continue to improve and that a brighter future lay ahead.

Nineteen thirty-six would be Arkansas' centennial year and preparations were under way to have a gala celebration throughout the state. Locally, there were plans to remodel several businesses on the square in Fayetteville and the Chamber of Commerce proposed that a City Hall, library and "centrally located" park should be high on Fayetteville's list of "to-dos" in 1936.

While these civic plans were being formulated, concerns about another of the town's enterprises—the Bears professional baseball club—were also being addressed. About six weeks prior to the turn of the new year, in what was becoming an annual rite, several local baseball men attended the yearly meeting of the NAPBL, ruling body of the minor leagues.

The convention, which began November 20, 1935, in Dayton, Ohio was attended by Charles Morgan, president of the Arkansas

Bernal Seamster
Photo courtesy of University of Arkansas Special Collections MC 637

State League, J. O. Clark, Rogers club president, Robert Henry, Siloam Springs club president, and Bernal Seamster, secretary of Fayetteville's franchise.

Besides going there to have a good time—the convention tended to "depart from formalities"—the area attendees were also very interested in finding financial backing for their struggling clubs and they hoped to get a good crop of ballplayers to fill out local team rosters as well.

Although club delegates from around the league would not actually meet on their own Northwest Arkansas turf until mid-January, one item of note was announced just before Christmas 1935. Homer "Doc" Ledbetter, formerly of both Fayetteville (1934) and Rogers (1935), was the Rogers Cardinals' choice as manager for the upcoming season.

At the formal January 15, 1936 mid-winter meeting of the Arkansas State League several important decisions were made. With noted baseball men like Tom Fairweather, long-time Western Association president, Al Eckert, president of the Springfield Cardinals, and Clifton A. "Runt" Marr, former president and manager of the Joplin Miners, attending, Charles Morgan resigned his league presidency due to business commitments. League secretary, Bernal Seamster, highly respected young lawyer and secretary of the Fayetteville club, was immediately elected to replace Morgan.

Among other topics discussed: whether Monett, Missouri, or Springdale would replace Huntsville, which was expected to give up its franchise; renaming the league if another Missouri club did come on board; and whether to have one or two official umpires work league games.

Backing for some clubs also was reported: Cassville already had the support of the Kansas City Blues of the AA American Association; Fayetteville, Siloam Springs and Rogers were to get help from higher leagues (though the teams were not yet announced); and Bentonville hoped to get backing but would try to run their team independently even if they did not.

Towards the end of January the Fayetteville Baseball Association, the administrative entity overseeing the Bears franchise, met in the offices of the Ozark Grocery Company to choose club executives and board members for the 1936 season.

Walter McWhorter was named president, Herman Tuck, vice-president, and Monroe Laner, secretary and treasurer. The board of directors, in addition to the three elected officers, consisted of Jerome McRoy, George Rogers, Jerry Lemarr, Bob Brown, C.W. (Dick) Trewhitt, R. D. Bogart, E. L. Wilson, Andrew Munding, Wallace Buxton, Bill Baggett, Walter Duggans, and Leland Bryan.

The next big news was reported February 10, 1936. League officials had met in Fayetteville the previous day and as expected awarded

Jim Bohart
Photo courtesy of University of Arkansas Special Collections MS L541

the forfeited Huntsville franchise to Monett, Missouri. With the addition of a second club from the Show-Me State, the circuit was officially renamed the Arkansas-Missouri League.

Adopting a new constitution and a new set of by-laws, the representatives also elected J. O. Clark of Rogers as vice president and Jim Bohart of Fayetteville as secretary to join recently elected president Bernal Seamster on the league's executive staff.

It was announced that Monett would pick up the same club sponsorship Huntsville had had from the Springfield Cardinals of the Western Association. Accordingly, Monett also retained the old club's nickname, the Red Birds. Rogers, it was revealed, would have the backing of the New York Yankees, via their Joplin Miners team in the Western Association, and Cassville, as earlier reported, would be sponsored by the Kansas City Blues of the American Association—also a Yankees farm club.

As winter progressed, so did preparations for the upcoming season. The Ray Doan baseball school, which included an adjunct school for umpires conducted by George Barr, opened February 15 in the mild climate of Hot Springs. Up north, Bentonville—still calling themselves the White Sox—signed Art Hauger, a veteran of 25 years in baseball, as their new manager.

In Fayetteville, work began on improvements to the Fair Grounds field and contracts were extended to holdover players from 1935, including Doug White, Allan Thomas, Paul Linch and Pete Negri. At the same time, a campaign was waged, notably by *Daily Democrat* sports writer, Al Williams, to bring back hometown boy Fred Hawn as manager of the local team.

1936 Season Schedule, Arkansas-Missouri League
Fayetteville Daily Democrat

At a meeting of Fayetteville club directors on March 2, the wish was granted and the "antediluvian" 28-year-old "ancient mariner" Hawn was named skipper of the 1936 Fayetteville Bears.[21] It was also announced that night that Cedar Rapids, the St. Louis Cardinals' Class A farm club from the Western League, would sponsor the Bears for the upcoming season.

On March 10, Fayetteville fans were invited out to the Fair Grounds to see the new wooden fence around the "smoothed" outfield. The *Daily Democrat* also explained that in 1936, each Arkansas-Missouri League team would be allowed to carry two veteran players as well as two class men. Veteran players were defined as having played two years in the Arkansas-Missouri (Arkansas State) League whereas class men were those with at least 10 games (hitters) or 54 innings (pitchers) in other leagues.

Saturday, March 21, it was reported that the Arkansas-Missouri League would play a 120 game schedule in 1936 starting May 7 and ending September 7. There would again be a split season, the first half ending July 5, with split season pennant winners (if no team won both halves) facing each other in a September playoff.

Because the cities were so close together, the league planned to have a unique set of double-headers on Sunday July 5 (the games ended up being played on Saturday July 4) in which the two teams involved (Fayetteville and Siloam Springs, for example) would play a morning game in one team's home park and then an afternoon contest at the other club's field.

Toward the end of March, manager Fred Hawn firmed up the Bears' pre-season practice plans. There would be a preliminary workout period from April 1 to April 22, wherein he would evaluate players—such as University of Arkansas students Willard "Lefty" Hawkins and Elmer Honea—specially invited to camp.

Hawn reported that 34 players had signed with the Bears and that about half of those were already going through drills. A few days later he went to Springfield, Missouri, to find more ballplayers and to chat with "Cap" Crossley, manager of the Cedar Rapids team sponsoring the Bears this season.

The following week, spring training began and Hawn had to cut his squad down to 28 players, including 17 pitchers, seven infielders and four outfielders. From this group would come the Fayetteville Bears of 1936.

Among the holdover players were Jim Jensen, Lawson Rinckey, and Troy Needham, pitchers; and Les Wilson, Pete Ashmore, and Doug White, infielders. Only Pete Negri was a returning outfielder. Among the notable new faces were Robert Olson and Dayton Lawson, pitchers; Paul Fugit and Barney Lutz in the infield; and Elmer Honea in the outfield.

Fayetteville had some special events lined up for spring training as the Bears had signed on to play both the Springfield Cardinals and the Joplin Miners of the Western Association in exhibition games at the Fair Grounds. Springfield—featuring Monty Johnson, the Bears second baseman from a year ago and Walker Cooper from the 1935 Rogers club—would get first crack at the Bears. Between 750 and 1,000 fans came out to the Fair Grounds Sunday, April 26, to see the locals get "drubbed" 30-9 by the visiting Cardinals.

The day after the Springfield-Fayetteville game, Arkansas-Missouri League president Bernal Seamster announced the league umpires would work in two-man crews: one-armed Jack Clemmens (retained from 1935) and Leonard Curtis; Don Streets and Lloyd Milton Seaman; Curtis B. Perryman and Lynn Kelley. Meanwhile, the Bears prepared for a hopefully more competitive game with the Joplin Miners.

Joplin, managed by famed ex-New York Yankee catcher Benny Bengough, featured ex-Arkansas State League players Bill Homan, Rogers second baseman in '34, and two Bentonville pitchers, also in '34—Joe Korach and Stroud Fields. Coming off a 22-11 doubling up of Monett, Joplin showed why Class C ball is better than Class D, giving the Bears a 12-2 thumping.

After those losses, the Bears managed to beat an independent Van Buren club twice during the next week and then, leading up to the May 7 opening day of the regular season, concluded spring training May 3 with "probably the best game ever played on the Fair Grounds diamond," defeating Rogers, now known as the Lions, in twelve innings.

Two days before the home opener, May 5, the Bears officially signed Willard Hawkins, a left-handed pitcher and University of Arkansas student. The team was also proud to point out, the *Daily Democrat* reported, that they would have two sets of uniforms in 1936, one for the road (color not specified) and the traditional "white togs" for home games.

"Bears Open League Season Thursday" proclaimed the front-page headline of the *Daily Democrat* for Wednesday, May 6, 1936.

Excitement about the new season was, as they might say in today's sports section, nearly "palpable." Baseball was the clear-cut national pastime, and it was time to play ball again.

The price of a ticket in Fayetteville had gone up to 30¢ for men this year while it was still 25¢ for women and 10¢ for kids. Siloam Springs was in town for the first game of the season, and the team nicknames, managers and sponsors were all set.

TEAM	NICKNAME	MANAGER	SPONSOR
Fayetteville	Bears	Fred Hawn	Cedar Rapids (Western League)
Siloam Springs	Travelers	Ray Powell	Cincinnati (National League)
Bentonville	Mustangs	Art Hauger	None
Rogers	Lions	Homer "Doc" Ledbetter	Joplin (Western Association)
Cassville	Blues	Gary Coker	Kansas City (Western Association)
Monett	Red Birds	Adolph Arlitt	Springfield (Western Association)[22]

In the opening game with Siloam Springs on May 7, Fayetteville's starters were:

Pete Negri	RF
Les Wilson	2B
Doug White	LF
Ed Kurkoski	CF
Barney Lutz	3B
Pete Ashmore	SS
Paul Fugit	1B
Fred Hawn	C
Lawson Rinckey	P

It was a thrilling season opener, too, as the Bears scored twice with two out in the bottom of the tenth inning to beat Siloam Springs 8-7 in front of 600-800 fans at the Fair Grounds. Pre-game festivities included a parade from the square out to the park; a performance by the Fayetteville High School band; and Judge Homer Jackson tossing out the first ball to Mayor A.D. McAllister.

Nothing in the pre-game show, however, could match the thrill fans had in watching Bears rookie Elmer Honea hit a pinch-hit, grand slam home run in his first professional at bat to help tie the score at 6-6 in the home half of the eighth inning. Siloam Springs scored in the top of the tenth to take a one run lead but the Bears came back to win by scoring twice with two out in the bottom of the inning. Pete Negri's last chance single proved to be the game winner.

The following day, Siloam Springs spanked the Bears 10-1 in front of 500 fans at the Travelers' home field, Smiley Park. Elsewhere, both Bentonville and Cassville won their first two games, over Rogers and Monett respectively, and the 1936 Arkansas-Missouri League season was off and running.

During the weekend, the Bears beat Siloam Springs again at the Fair Grounds, and then on Sunday, winless Monett became winless no more, topping the Bears before 800 faithful Fayetteville fans. In that game, the Bears set a league record by leaving 16 runners stranded on base.

During the first ten days of the season, the talk of the the league wasn't the play of the Bears, the news was the Cassville Blues. The Blues won their first seven games of the year and threatened to leave the rest of the league behind. Finally, on May 15, Bentonville stopped the Blues at Cassville, but the Missourians continued winning at an impressive rate.

Meanwhile, the Bears won some and lost some. Then, towards the middle of the month they lost four in a row—including three straight to Bentonville—before defeating league-leading Cassville May 19 at the Fair Grounds. Elmer Honea hit his fifth home run of the young season and Blues manager Gary Coker was tossed out of the game by umpire Jack Clemmens for arguing a called strike on the very last Blues batter.

The paper also reported that last year's league leading hitter, Duane (Dee) Kratzer of Cassville (now with Albany of the Georgia-Florida League), would receive the Spalding Trophy for having the nation's highest average (a remarkable .397) for a rookie in 1935.

Two days later an alliterative *Daily Democrat* headline read: *"Blues Bunch Blows Beating Bears, 9-8."* The next day Cassville followed that win up with another victory over Fayetteville this time before a week-day crowd of 400 at the Fair Grounds. With the season a little over two weeks old, the Missourians had a solid hold on first place.

After the Cassville series, the Bears went to Siloam Springs where the Travelers greeted them with an eleven-run first inning then held on as the Bears came roaring back to score six runs in the fifth inning and nine more in the last three to come up one run short in a 17-16 loss Friday, May 22.

After beating the Travelers back home on Saturday, the Bears ran into a pitching buzz saw by the name of Johnny (Al) Murray who four-hit the Bears 4-0 in a quick one hour and twenty-five minute Sunday tilt at Siloam Springs that knocked the Bears into last place in the league. Barney Lutz, Bears rightfielder, had his 15 game hitting streak stopped by Murray. Lutz had hit safely in every game of the season up to then.

As the Bears stumbled into the basement, they looked for some pitching help, adding pitchers Walker Henderson and Kenyon "Red" Cross[23] to their staff. They also added outfielder Robert Million to the club and got an immediate payback on their investments, a home win over Monett on May 27 that snapped a four game losing streak.

Elsewhere around the league, it was learned that Clifford Clay had replaced Gary Coker on May 27 as manager of the league-leading Cassville Blues. Clay immediately pitched Cassville to a victory over Rogers, knocking out two home runs and a single just for good measure.

The next afternoon in Fayetteville, a Merchant's Day crowd of 1500 saw the "cellar dwelling" Bears beat Rogers. It was the fourth straight home game played in one hour and forty-five minutes or less. The Bears might not have been playing good baseball, but at least at home they were playing it really fast.

Going just as fast in another direction, Bentonville kept winning game after game. When they beat Monett on May 29, the Mustangs overtook Cassville for the league lead. Losing two to Rogers on the last weekend of May, Fayetteville's Bears entered June dead last in the league.

One bright spot for Fayetteville continued to be the power hitting of University of Arkansas junior agriculture student Elmer Honea. The first set of league statistics (for games through May 24) showed Honea tied for league home run honors, 6, with Cassville's Woody Fair.

Back on the ballfields, Fayetteville went to Cassville on June 2 and beat the Blues in eleven innings to hand Cassville their fifth straight loss while the Bears stopped a losing streak of their own at three. Bentonville, meanwhile, beat Rogers at home to win their eighth in a row. The next afternoon, with Elmer Honea out taking a final exam at the University, the Bears lost to the Cassville Blues and also lost Fred Hawn to a sprained wrist sustained when he "unnecessarily" slid into home.

In the next few days the Bears had some interesting games. They took a 15-2 "lacing" at Cassville, June 4, but followed that by twice beating league leader, Bentonville, whose recent win streak had been ended by Rogers at nine in a row. But then, "upholding a reputation of playing their worst before big crowds," the Bears were pummeled 20-6 in front of 1,000 fans at the Fair Grounds, June 7, by those same Mustangs.

The June 11 edition of the *Fayetteville Daily Democrat*, celebrating the state's one-hundredth birthday, was extraordinary. Not only was the paper itself filled with general historical information and the news that President Franklin Delano Roosevelt had come to Hot Springs to be part of the celebration, but there was also a special centennial section providing detailed articles on state, county, city and citizen history. As for the Bears, they were in Siloam Springs that day winning a 6-2 decision over the Travelers.

Leading up to mid-month, the Bears lost to Siloam Spring's Clint Raper; then stopped Travelers ace Johnny (Al) Murray's personal pitching win streak at eight; and beat the Travelers again on June 14. At this point in the season, Cassville had regained the top spot in the league.

Through the rest of the first half of the season, the Bears basically played .500 ball going 11-10, but they hit the ball very well. On June 21, Bears shortstop Pete Ashmore tied the league record for consecutive hits (8) and set a league record by going eight for eight in a double-header the Bears split at Monett.

In the second game of that double-header—a 5-0 loss—Les Wilson of the Bears went 0 for 3 to end a remarkable twenty-game hitting streak. Fred Hawn, the Bears "portly" manager-catcher, who had hit in ten straight games himself when Wilson was finally stopped, continued his own streak until the first week of the second half of the season.

In a Bears win over Rogers on June 25 at the Fair Grounds—the first of a three game sweep of Rogers and of a four game win skein overall—a peculiar incident occurred on the visitors' very last at bat.

With two out in the top of the ninth, Ed O'Connell, the Lions first baseman, hit what appeared to be the game-tying home run. The ball, however, bounced back from the stands and into play. Bears outfielders claimed it hit off the top of the fence, while other witnesses believed it hit beyond the "barrier" and somehow ricocheted back onto the playing field. Whatever the ball had done out in the field,

O'Connell was jogging along in his home run trot when the hustling Bears outfielders relayed the ball to the plate to put out the startled Rogers would-be-hero.

Elsewhere in the league, Bobby Neighbors of Siloam Springs set a league mark with four home runs in a June 21 double-header with Bentonville. Neighbors hit three of the home runs in game one—in consecutive innings.

In Cassville, player-manager Clifford Clay, after having pitched a two-hit, 10-0 gem of a game against Monett on June 16, came unraveled. Umpires threw Clay out of Cassville's home loss to Fayetteville on June 19 and the next day in Fayetteville, Clay stormed off the pitcher's mound in frustration during an 18-6 beating the Blues took from the Bears.

The result of Clay's antics was that, on June 24, it was announced he had "stepped down" as Cassville's manager and that Erwin "Zeke" Gansauer, also a pitcher, who was in his second year with Cassville, would become the new Blues team leader.

In Fayetteville, although the Bears had stumbled at the end of the first half in losing five of their last six games, the league's home and away Fourth of July double-header concept (originally set for Sunday, July 5) went off reasonably well.

Playing in Siloam Springs for the morning game on Independence Day, the Bears beat the Travelers 7-6. Then in the afternoon game, the Bears—giving "a miserable account of themselves before a big … afternoon crowd"—were defeated by the Travelers at Fayetteville's Fair Grounds 15-2.

Elsewhere, Bentonville and Rogers also split their doubleheader (leaving the 1934 and 1935 champs in last place), as did Cassville and Monett, although Cassville's game one win clinched the first half pennant for the tiny Blues franchise.

Fayetteville closed out the first half season on July 5 with a loss to the new champions from Cassville.

The final first half standings were as follows:

Arkansas-Missouri League
(Final standings—first half)

Team	Won	Lost	Pct.
Cassville	36	24	.600
Bentonville	33	26	.559
Siloam Springs	31	27	.534
Monett	28	32	.467
Fayetteville	26	34	.433
Rogers	24	35	.407

A hopeful group of Fayetteville Bears and their long-suffering fans began the season's second half July 8 on an upbeat note, a win over Cassville at the Fair Grounds, despite the Blues pulling the league's second triple play of 1936.

One member of the Fair Grounds crowd that day was Doc Ledbetter, who had just been relieved of his player-manager duties by last-place Rogers. The Lions then signed Frank Stapleton, who had guided them during the second half of their 1935 championship season, as their new on-field leader. The team promptly won its first game under Stapleton at Monett. As for Doc Ledbetter, he wasn't unemployed long; Bentonville traded for him the following day.

After losing to Cassville on July 9 (Fred Hawn's nineteen-game hitting streak would end the next day), Fayetteville's Bears then reeled off four straight wins to be alone in first place on July 14.

During that winning first week of the second half, Elmer Honea hit home runs in four of five games from July 8 through July 12, only missing during a win over Rogers on July 11. The most explosive win was the last one, on July 13, a twenty-two hit, 14-4 victory again at Rogers.

Once again, however, being on top proved to be the Bears' downfall. They promptly lost nine straight games. The first, on July 14, at home to Siloam Springs and the last—also at home on July 22—to Bentonville When the bad run ended the Bears were dead last in the league.

Writing for the *Daily Democrat,* Walter J. Lemke compared the Bears losing streak to the current drought in the region. "One of 'em," he quipped, "will have to crack soon." The baseball streak broke before the weather did.

On July 23, the Bears beat Cassville at the Fair Grounds behind the pitching of re-signed prodigal son "Hornbuckle Buck" Buchanan, who had been a mainstay on the team back in the Fayetteville Educators days. The Bears also re-signed pitcher, Russell "Lefty" Poole, another leftover from Educators days, and released another southpaw, Willard "Lefty" Hawkins.

In other league news, Siloam Springs pulled out to a comfortable lead over the other clubs behind the pitching of Johnny Murray (who was doing so well he was sold for $200 to the El Dorado Lions of the Class C Cotton States League after his fifteenth victory on July 25) and Clint Raper.

On July 17, Monett announced that Ken Blackman, a former manager in the league, would take over leadership of the Red Birds from Buzz Arlitt who continued as the team's first baseman. Monett proceeded to go on an eight-game winning streak to stay within striking distance of league-leader Siloam Springs.

With July sliding into August, Fayetteville managed to play well enough to be a couple of games over .500, at least during a twelve-game span. A highlight during this stretch was Elmer Honea's outstanding, and dangerous, catch in a victory at Cassville July 24. The Bears outfielder caught a fly ball "close to the *stone* (my emphasis) wall in deep center" of the Missouri ballpark.

Around the league, Siloam Springs won ten straight games (tying their own league record set in 1934) and Bentonville won seven in a row. Monett lost six in a row and when the dust cleared, Siloam Springs was still well out in front in the second-half pennant race.

Individual highlights included the Siloam Springs pitcher, Clint Raper, improving his record to a sterling 17-5 and Rudolph "Woody" Tone (an All-Star in the league in both 1934 and 1935 as Rudolph Woodrow), Raper's teammate, hitting for the cycle (the rare occurrence in which a player hits a single, double, triple, and home run in one game) in a win over Monett at Siloam Springs. In Rogers, "old" one-eyed Pete Casey returned to the league, signing on to catch for the Lions.

About the time it was reported Jesse Owens had won his third championship at the 1936 Berlin Olympics (August 5)—the *Daily Democrat* sports page had stories accusing Bentonville players of being the "worst umpire baiters in the circuit" and reporting that Fayetteville fans wished their raggedy team would launder their dirt-coated uniforms—the Bears began another nose dive in the league, losing eight of their next nine games.

This time they really had bad luck, on and off the field. The bad play at home "jinx" held especially true on August 10 at the Fair Grounds where, despite Paul Fugit's seventh successful hidden-ball-trick of the season, which caught a Red Birds runner off first for an easy out in the second inning, the Bears lost to Monett, 3-1.

The night before, on their way home from the only win during the losing streak, at Monett, the Bears' bus was stopped in Springdale and "raided" by state revenue officers who confiscated cigarettes purchased in Missouri and ordered the poor bus driver to appear in court on bond.

The worst news, though, was that the Bears outstanding first baseman Paul Fugit, the "Wichita Kid" as Walter Lemke called him, was suffering from attacks of appendicitis. On Wednesday, August 12, the popular Fugit was out of the lineup and that night underwent an appendectomy at Fayetteville City Hospital. Although the first baseman was lost for the season, Bears fans were relieved to learn that the operation was successful and that Fugit would fully regain his health.

Over this bad stretch and through four more games that the Bears split with Monett and Bentonville, the roster took its usual beating. A recent signee, outfielder Dave Smith, was released and, to take his and other open slots, the Bears signed two more golden oldies from Educators days: Cline Watson and Jake Drake, though neither player participated in many games. Richard "Dick" Bohl, from Siloam Springs and property of the Cincinnati Reds, was signed to play first base in Fugit's absence.

As for Siloam Springs, the Travelers were playing so well, with

Clint Raper reeling off win after win, that even a Bentonville streak in which the Mustangs won nine of ten wasn't enough to dislodge the league leaders. On August 18, in a crucial series between the two teams, Raper shut out Bentonville's Ponies 3-0 with a five-hitter to claim win number twenty on the season. The victory was Raper's tenth in a row, tying the league record set by Rogers' Cotton Hill in 1935.

On August 19, happily, the Bears took off on a five-game winning streak beginning with a victory over Rogers at the Fair Grounds. Then, helping the "coming" Bentonville Mustangs gain ground on the league leaders, the Bears beat Siloam Springs three games in a row.

In the first Siloam Springs game, the Bears' "Red" Cross took the win over Clint Raper, the league's best pitcher, whose consecutive win streak was ended at ten. The Bears fifth win in the streak was a victory in Rogers. To complete the team's good run, Paul Fugit was released from the hospital and reported to be "recovering very fast" in his room at 521 N. College.

The upshot of the Bears win skein, especially those over Siloam Springs, was to tighten the league race. When Bentonville beat Siloam Springs on Sunday, August 23, the Ponies were within two and one-half games of the struggling Travelers. It was, however, to be as close as Bentonville would get.

For the next week or so after the win streak, Fayetteville played slightly sub-.500 ball, going 3-4. They beat Bentonville at the Fair Grounds August 25 in front of 350 fans on "Bears Appreciation Night," and two days later, defeated the Ponies 16-0 in front of a much larger crowd on the last Merchants' Day promotion of the year. Kenyon "Red" Cross got the victory, pitching the Bears' first shutout of the season. Three days later on August 30, big Robert Olson pitched a 4-0 shutout against the Cassville Blues.

On August 26, the league All-Star team was announced, but Fayetteville placed no one on the first team. They were, however, very well represented in the Honorable Mention category as Paul Fugit, Les Wilson, Doug White, Pete Ashmore, Elmer Honea, Fred Hawn, Barney Lutz, and Earl Smalling were all chosen for that honor.

On a humorous note, Walter Lemke, writing as "Uncle Walt" Lemke in the *Daily Democrat*, noted that Fayetteville batboy Sherm Lollar's uniform had become so worn late in the season that the kid had to patch it up with adhesive tape.

A proper lady fan, Lemke wrote, suggested most vigorously that the young man's disgraceful uniform should at the very least be sewed up. Lollar, however, would have to wait a few years to wear really good uniforms—that would be during the 1950s when he became a slugging Major League All-Star catcher for the Chicago White Sox.

September 3 was Fred Hawn Day at the Fair Grounds in Fayetteville and the Bears manager and catcher received an automatic shotgun from Mayor A.D. McAllister in appreciation of Hawn's efforts during the year. Unfortunately the Bears lost to Monett on Hawn's day and the hard luck backstop-pilot also took a foul tip off his finger and was lost for the remaining games of the season.

On Saturday, September 5, Elmer Honea hit his twentieth home run of the year in a loss to Rogers and in the season finale, a win Monday, September 7 over Rogers at the Fair Grounds in front of one of the largest weekday crowds of the year, Barney Lutz played all nine positions in the field for the Bears, one inning at each spot, giving up only one run during his inning as a pitcher.

A remarkable event occurred in the Bears' next to last game, a Sunday, September 6 victory over Cassville at the Fair Grounds. In that game, Farmington's Frances "Sonny" Dunlap, an All-American basketball player and sister of local sports star Buster Dunlap, played the entire game in right field for the Bears.

Frances, who was a nationally known star for the Tulsa Stenos women's AAU basketball club, had tried out for the U.S. Olympic team and was without doubt one of the finest athletes to ever come out of northwest Arkansas.

For the Bears that day, Frances had no chances in right field—though she was reported to have given a "swell account of herself" at third base during infield practice—and she went 0 for 3 at bat. She did made contact on all three trips to the plate, however, and in one at bat forced Cassville leftfielder Gene McCarty to "make a nice running catch" to get her out. It is believed that Frances was probably "the first girl in history to play an entire game of organized baseball."

At Siloam Springs the Travelers had already clinched the second-half pennant for the second year in a row with a win over Fayetteville on manager Ray Powell Day, September 2. Powell received a watch from the Siloam Springs fans for his work with the local team. A few days earlier, Rogers manager, Frank "Buck" Stapleton, had received a traveling bag from the Rogers faithful. Mired in last place and in the throes of a nine-game losing streak, the Lions did themselves proud by sweeping a double-header from Monett.

In Monett, they had Buzz Arlitt Day on the last day of the season (September 7) and the giant first first baseman—"a popular figure all over the league"—received a gold watch. Before some 800 home fans, the Red Birds then won a "dramatic" 2-0 decision over Cassville when Woody Fair hit a two-run home run in the bottom of the eighth inning.

As for the Bears, they closed out the last week of the 1936 season by winning three of their last four games, including a final day home win over Rogers, to finish solidly in fourth place. The final regular season standings were as follows:

Arkansas-Missouri League
(Final standings—second half)

Team	Won	Lost	Pct.
Siloam Springs	43	17	.717
Bentonville	36	23	.610
Monett	28	31	.475
Fayetteville	27	33	.450
Cassville	25	35	.417
Rogers	20	40	.333

The 1936 Arkansas-Missouri League championship playoff series was between Siloam Springs and first-half winner Cassville. The plan was to have a best 5 of 9 series and Cassville, with a small park and therefore smaller crowds, requested and received permission to play their "home" games in Monett, Fayetteville (where the announced season attendance of 12,000 had led the league) and Rogers.

Possibly catching the second-half champions off guard, tiny Cassville took a one game to none lead in the series by beating the Travelers at Siloam Springs on September 9, even managing to defeat ace pitcher Clint Raper. Next day the two teams battled to a 14-inning tie at Monett in a game called by darkness.

Electing not to finish that game, the series went back to Siloam Springs where the Travelers evened the series with a win. Kermit Lewis, who had an all-time league record 28 home runs during the regular season, hit another one on this day for the winners.

Siloam Springs won the next game on September 13 before 1,200 fans at Fayetteville—without Clint Raper who had run "afoul" of training regulations—and followed up with a win at home to lead the series 3 games to 1.

Cassville came back the next game (September 15 at Rogers) to win behind manager Erwin "Zeke" Gansauer, who not only sealed the victory in relief but also received a watch from appreciative Cassville fans. The Blues followed that win with a victory at Siloam Springs the next day to square the series at three games apiece.

After two straight days of rain, it was agreed to cut the series to a best four out of seven format and have the remaining game played Sunday, September 20, in Fayetteville. Unfortunately, it began raining that day in Fayetteville, too, so the teams loaded up their buses, the fans followed in their cars, and the championship game was played in Rogers.

Before the "largest crowd" the Rogers park had ever held, Siloam Springs claimed the 1936 crown with a 5-1 victory behind Clint Raper's pitching.

In the final statistics for the year, Raper had ended with an excellent 23-7 record. Teammate Kermit Lewis, the home run king, had come in second in league hitting with a .3326 average, losing to batting champion Les Rock of Bentonville who edged out the Siloam Springs slugger with a mark of .3333—a remarkably close difference of only .0007.

With that very tight batting race and the fine playoff series between Siloam Springs and Cassville concluded, the full and action-packed 1936 Arkansas-Missouri League season came to an end.

FIVE
1937: Angels in the Ozarks

BETWEEN THE END of the 1936 season and the start of spring training in April, 1937, the Arkansas-Missouri League continued its well-established pattern of dynamic change. While events of national and international import occurred—President Roosevelt was re-elected and hurried off to a peace conference in Argentina with Secretary of State Cordell Hull in attendance, the Spanish Civil War blazed on, and King Edward of England abdicated his throne to marry an American commoner—this small, backwater, Class D minor league made ready for its fourth year of play.

In the fall of 1936, Arkansas-Missouri League officials voted to raise the total monthly player salary limit to $1000 and adopt a 110-game schedule. They also decided to abandon the split-season format in favor of the "Shaughnessy" playoff system in which the top four teams play each other to determine the leauge champion.

As the new year rolled around, league president Bernal Seamster of Fayetteville, re-elected for his second consecutive term, was faced with two major problems: replacing Cassville, Missouri and Bentonville—both franchises had folded during the winter—and finding sponsorship for both new and surviving clubs.

For the four returning teams, sponsorship seemed solid by early January. Siloam Springs was to be backed by the St. Louis Browns, Rogers by the New York Yankees, Monett by Springfield, Missouri (a St. Louis Cardinals farm club), and Fayetteville by Cedar Rapids, Iowa—also a Cardinals team.

Finding two new clubs to fill out the proposed six-team loop took a while longer, but by early February 1937, Neosho, Missouri, had filled the fifth slot. The remaining team—possibly Miami, Oklahoma or Springdale it was speculated—had yet to be determined.

Meanwhile, Fayetteville—which was "determined to keep baseball" in the city—faced its usual financial difficulties. Even though the Bears had drawn over 12,000 fans at the Fair Grounds in 1936 and had a gate increase of $500 more than in 1935, the franchise was still short of funds for the upcoming season.

On February 18, the club was $335 shy of the $1200 minimum required to operate the team. A drive was launched to raise the money from local fans and businesses and it proved successful. By March 1, Jim Bohart—*Fayetteville Daily Democrat* Sports Editor—reported that the 1937 Arkansas-Missouri League season, including Fayetteville once again, was a done deal.

March also brought the signing of two managers in the league: Ted Mayer at Rogers and Fred Hawn—probably the most popular and revered baseball figure in Fayetteville—who would be back at the helm of the local club. While Hawn spent the next month selecting players for spring training and evaluating them in camp, league president Seamster—at the behest of the other franchises—finally invited Vinita, Oklahoma to join the loop on April 11.

With six teams now assumed to be set, spring training went into full swing. Bears holdovers Paul Fugit and Barney Lutz were among two dozen players vying for spots on the 1937 team. Towards the end of the month the Bears beat Rogers in the first exhibition game of the year and the 1937 schedule was printed in the *Daily Democrat*. The new schedule included Vinita as one of the six clubs in the league.

As April turned into May it was learned that Neosho, the newest team in the league, would introduce night games during the season and would call themselves, appropriately enough, the Nighthawks. In Fayetteville, the club announced that OK and Milady Cleaners would provide a clubhouse for the players and that ticket prices would be 35¢ for men, 25¢ for women and a dime for kids. To round things off, the

Bears beat Rogers again in another exhibition game. Then on May 4, the *Daily Democrat* reported that Fayetteville's Bears were no more.

Back on March 22, a barely noticed story in the *Democrat* had told how Fayetteville purchased two sets of hand-me-down uniforms from Ponca City, Oklahoma, of the Class C Western Association. Now, with only two days left until opening day, it was revealed to the public that the "new" uniforms had "lettered in script on the beautiful 100% wool"[24] shirts the name "Angels."

Club officials called an immediate, emergency meeting. Could they afford to remove the name Angels "stitch by stitch" from every shirt and sew Bears on them instead? Given the club's usual financial situation, the directors said no way—"Why go to the expense?" one of them was quoted as saying—and so the Bears were quickly and unceremoniously renamed the Angels. It was the team's third nickname in its four-year existence but it would be their last and the one by which they would be remembered.

May 5, the very next day after the Angels came into being and the day before the Arkansas-Missouri League was to begin its season, fans and officials were stunned by the news that Vinita would not field a team after all. It was a real bombshell of an announcement and the loss of the Oklahoma club created a scheduling dilemma.

The league was determined to go on, however, even if doing so with an uneven number of teams was virtually, if not totally, unheard of. Some thought was given to going back to four teams but the new Neosho franchise promised to be such a solid one that the league decided to simply regroup and reschedule.

Making a new schedule for a five-team league was a daunting, unparalleled task, but Bernal Seamster of Fayetteville and Robert Henry, president of the Siloam Springs team, put their heads together and pulled it off.[25]

Taking advantage of the proximity of league towns to one another and Neosho's ability to hold night games at their park, the schedule-makers kept the five teams busy by setting up lots of seven-inning double-headers and frequent night visits to Neosho. This would mean more traveling, of course. For example, Fayetteville might drive to Monett for an afternoon game and then have to head on to Neosho for a night contest, but the new complicated schedule worked and kept the league alive.

Despite the loss of Vinita and the ensuing scheduling snafu, the 1937 Arkansas-Missouri League season managed to get off to an on time, if shaky, start. While most of the world was reeling from the tragedy of the Hindenburg disaster, which dominated the news of May 7, Fayetteville opened the year with a far less momentous win at Rogers.

In the other opening-day game, Monett won at Neosho. Because the new schedule had not yet been worked out, it fell to Siloam Springs to be the odd, fifth team out on the first day of the new season.

After a one-day delay due to rain, Fayetteville lost its home opener to Rogers in front of 750 fans at the Fair Grounds. The Angels starting lineup for the opener looked like this:

Elmer Poss	CF
Bob McCarron	3B
Paul Fugit	1B
Barney Lutz	RF
Jim Van Wey	C
Earl Naylor,	LF
Kenneth Meyer	SS
Dan Jarvis	2B
Edward Smith	P

As they had in other years, local merchants offered various prizes to Angels players for selected "firsts" of the season. Bob McCarron, for example, took in $1 in cash from the American Legion-DAV Snooker Parlor for making the team's first error; Earl Naylor made the first put-out and received a carton of cigarettes from the Ozark Grocery; and second baseman Dan Jarvis got a case of Coca-Cola from the Fayetteville Ice Company for hitting the Angels' first home run.

Once the season got rolling, the Angels played much like the Educators and the Bears had before them: inconsistently. In the first ten days they went 4-5, winning that opener at Rogers, losing five straight, then winning three in a row. A familiar story to locals.

In Rogers, the Lions started fast, winning seven in a row in a stretch that featured a three home run outburst in a single game at Monett by Lions second baseman Gerry Priddy, a future major leaguer with the New York Yankees.

Siloam Springs, meanwhile, acted like the Angels: they lost their first four, then won four in a row. Monett just played poorly, but after another Fayetteville loss at Rogers on May 18, the Angels actually fell behind everyone into last place.

Yet, in the topsy-turvy early going, only three days later, Fayetteville had moved up to third in the league. Through the rest of May, the Angels were one game over .500 and ended the first month of the season in fourth place only one-half game out of third and just three shy of first place Rogers.

The first week of June was excellent for Fayetteville as they went 5-1, including their first victory over Neosho. They won four of these games in just two days with road victories over Monett and Neosho on June 3, followed by June 4 Fair Grounds wins against Neosho (again) and Rogers to pull within one-half game of league leading Rogers. During this same spell, the less fortunate Monett club stumbled through a twelve-game losing streak and was mired in last place in the league.

In non-baseball news from around the country, Amelia Earhart took off from Miami, Florida on what would end up being her last flying trip—"around the world just for fun"—and former University of Arkansas All-Southwest Conference football and basketball star Ike Poole was arrested in Corpus Christi, Texas in the shooting death of an out-of-uniform Texas state traffic officer. Less than a week later, however, a grand jury ruled that Poole had acted in self-defense and the ex-Razorback was freed after all charges against him were dropped.

Ike Poole
Photo courtesy of University of Arkansas Special Collections MS L541

As for the Angels, after their brief positive surge, they began a skid, going 3-6 through the middle of June including a loss to Rogers in front of 1,000 home fans on June 6. They broke a four-game losing streak June 14, beating Monett at the Fair Grounds, with the help of Doc Ledbetter, who once again had re-signed with the team. Also here early in the new season, the Fayetteville Baseball Association purchased the Fair Grounds ballpark and continued their plans—aided by the Lions Club—to bring night baseball to town.

Through the rest of June the Angels played even worse than they had earlier. The team stumbled along, winning only four of thirteen games—including losing streaks of five and then four games. When they did win, it was due to outstanding pitching.

On June 16, Maurice "Babe" Chartrand tossed a two-hitter in shutting out Siloam Springs; Ed Smith struck out 16 batters in a win at Neosho June 19; Albert White, new of Monett, two-hit his old teammates June 23 at the Fair Grounds; and then Dick Burse pitched a one-hitter at Monett in an Angels victory on June 27.

For the Angels the biggest news of the month, or probably of the year for that matter, came on Friday, June 25. On that evening, thanks to a 100,000-watt flood lighting system sponsored by the Lions Club, the dream of night baseball became a reality in Fayetteville.

A minor glitch delayed the start of the contest by ten minutes, but when the lights were switched on 1,250 fans were treated to the first home night game in the history of the Fayetteville franchise. In twelve innings, the Angels lost to archrival Rogers. Playing under the arc lights must have been difficult for the players that first night, because the two teams committed ten errors between them, six by the visiting Lions.

When July began, the Angels found themselves entrenched in fourth place. As the club usually did when it was struggling, which traditionally had been often, it made roster changes. Catcher Jim Van Wey and second baseman Dan Jarvis were released to make way for Mark Hodgson and Jake Nabor who picked up the same positions, respectively. The team responded with a six-game winning streak. At home on July 1 they beat Neosho in the afternoon and then defeated Rogers to gain their first night game victory anywhere.

While the Angels reeled off their wins, Siloam Springs was doing even better, winning seven games in a row and twelve of fourteen overall to take the league lead. Two days after Siloam Springs' seventh straight victory, on July 3, Arkansas—really, the United States at large—was stunned at the news of the loss of Amelia Earhart who, as reported in the *Daily Democrat,* had been lost at sea somewhere in the vast reaches of the South Pacific.

On the Fourth of July, 850 fans watched the Angels defeat Rogers

Jim Van Wey
Photo courtesy of Powers Museum, Carthage, Missouri

at the Fair Grounds while in Siloam Springs, Walt Ward and LeRoy Youngblood of Monett combined for a 1-0 seven-inning no-hitter, the second no-hit game in league history, against the first place Travelers.

Monday, July 5, the *Fayetteville Daily Democrat* announced that it was going to change its name to the *Northwest Arkansas Times* and did so with the Thursday, July 8, 1937 edition.[26] That day, the Angels won for the eighth time in nine games, beating Neosho at the Fair Grounds and also tying a league record by turning five double plays in the contest. On Friday, July 9, Rogers played and won its first night game at home by beating Siloam Springs in front of 1,642 paying customers.

The next big news in the league involved a "trifecta" change of managers. Fred Hawn, the Angels' manager, was promoted to New Iberia, Louisiana in the larger Class D Evangeline League. To replace Hawn, Fayetteville raided lowly Monett and signed their manager Ken Blackman. Joe Davis, managing at Midland in the West-Texas New Mexico League, became the new manager in Monett. Under Blackman, Fayetteville won their first three games and the new manager even hit a home run in his first game, a ten inning victory over Neosho at the Fair Grounds on July 13.

On Friday, July 16, Siloam Springs held their first ever night game, a win against Monett (only Monett was now left without a lighted field) in front of 1,000 fans. Fayetteville lost at Rogers that same evening to bring their fourth place record to .500 (37-37).

Fayetteville was far back in the league standings at that point, eight and one-half games out of first place, but then, unexpectedly they suddenly turned into winners. With new manager, Blackman, at the helm, the Angels ran off eight consecutive wins.

On Sunday, July 18, they won two games at the Fair Grounds, beating ex-Angel Babe Chartrand and Monett in the first half of a mixed-team doubleheader and then defeating Rogers in the second contest. The next night, they beat another ex-Angel, Albert White at Rogers and on July 21, the night after Monett's new manager, Joe Davis, pitched a one-hit shutout to beat Siloam Springs 3-0, the Angels scored ten runs in the sixth inning of their game to beat Neosho (which had lost ten straight during this stretch) 10-8 at the Fair Grounds.

When the ashes settled at the end of the month, Fayetteville had won seventeen of twenty-one ball games under Ken Blackman and was solidly in second place, three and one-half games behind front-running Rogers. During this extraordinary streak, old favorites Jake Drake and Buck Buchanan had re-signed with the team, and for the first time, Fayetteville had what it had never had before—a winning team.

The standings at the end of July were as follows:

Arkansas-Missouri League
(Standings—July 31, 1937)

Team	Won	Lost	Pct.
Rogers	56	38	.596
Fayetteville	51	40	.560
Siloam Springs	47	45	.511
Neosho	44	46	.489
Monett	29	58	.333

With the arrival of August, however, the Angels stumbled a bit and during the first ten days of the month went 5-7. The play of the team was overshadowed, however, by the tragic death of one of the league's most respected men: veteran player, manager and, of late, umpire, Pete Casey.

On Thursday, August 5, Casey died in Rogers of a self-inflicted gunshot wound. Apparently distraught over an impending divorce from his wife Maud—who was in Denver at the time—Casey walked into his lawyer's office on Tuesday, August 3 and shot himself in the stomach with a revolver.

A native of Bentonville, Casey—who managed Fayetteville during the first half of 1935—had once had a promising baseball career until an errant pitch left him with only one good eye. On Friday, August 6, fans and players throughout the Arkansas-Missouri League paused for a moment of silence in respect for their fallen comrade.

Back in league play, Fayetteville suffered their first home loss under manager Blackman to Siloam Springs at the Fair Grounds on the day Pete Casey died. The next night they lost the second half of a home doubleheader 1-0 to Rogers. It was Rogers' eighth straight win and a tough loss for the Angels' Ed Smith who had pitched a no-hit game until Lions catcher Augie Navarro hit a home run in the top of the ninth (of a scheduled seven-inning contest) for the victory.

On Sunday, August 8, Fayetteville fans witnessed another performance by Frances Dunlap, local star female athlete, who played five innings at second base for the Angels. This year Frances got a hit, going

1 for 2 at bat, including a single and a strikeout. She played flawlessly in the field, handling four chances—including two line drives—without an error.

The next night, Fayetteville lost to Rogers at the Fair Grounds to fall nine and one-half games behind the Lions, but then the second-place Angels began the longest winning streak in franchise history. The club won ten straight.

During the streak they defeated Siloam Springs four times and Neosho five. They finally lost to Rogers in Fayetteville, August 21, to end the streak, but defeated Siloam Springs 1-0 the next day (Angel shortstop Ken "Buddy" Meyer stole home for the game's only run) to win for the eleventh time in twelve games.

But for all their success, the Angels were still in second place and had only gained two and one-half games in the standings, leaving them seven full games behind the Rogers Lions who had won over two-thirds of their games to stem Fayetteville's charge. On Monday, August 23, Fayetteville lost twice, during the day at Rogers and then at Neosho in the evening. Fayetteville's second loss that day gave Rogers the 1937 Arkansas-Missouri League regular-season pennant outright.

Despite not being able to catch Rogers, Fayetteville had had an extraordinary run of victories during those last weeks leading up to the playoffs. From the time Ken Blackman took charge of the club in mid-July, until the team's hot run ended late in August, the Angels went 33-12, winning at an extraordinary .733 clip. They even won an exhibition game over Rogers on August 16 before 750 fans at the Fair Grounds in a contest designed to give the players some extra money ($165 was divided evenly between the two squads).

On August 21, league All-Stars were announced and Fayetteville dominated the squad with five players selected to the first team: Paul Fugit, First Base; Bob McCarron, Third Base; Barney Lutz, Right Field; Loy Hanning, Right-Handed Pitcher; and manager Ken Blackman, Utility Player. In addition, Jack Troupe, Earl Naylor, Ed Smith and Andy Sinay of the Angels made Honorable Mention.

With the regular season race already decided, Fayetteville played without enthusiasm in their last ten contests, going 3-7. One of the losses was an eighteen-inning marathon defeat at Siloam Springs on August 25, which was the longest game in Arkansas-Missouri League history lasting a full four hours and ten minutes. The next night the Angels beat Monett in eleven innings at the Fair Grounds and the fans gave Ken Blackman a wrist watch for his fine job of managing the club.

The team closed out the season by losing their last three games, but the playoffs were all set. Rogers and Neosho would play each other in one best of five series while Fayetteville and Siloam Springs would contend in the other, with the winners to meet for the league championship.

The final standings for 1937 were as follows:

Arkansas-Missouri League
(Final Standings)

Team	Won	Lost	Pct.
Rogers	79	48	.622
Fayetteville	70	56	.556
Siloam Springs	66	61	.520
Neosho	52	71	.423
Monett	45	76	.372

The playoffs began August 30 with the Angels defeating Siloam Springs at the Fair Grounds before 650 fans. In Rogers, the Lions opened their series with a home victory over Neosho. The next day Fayetteville won at Siloam Springs and on September 1, after being feted at a Lion's Club luncheon, they beat the Travelers again to sweep the series three games to none in front of 1,000 home fans.

Rogers took an extra game to join the Angels in the championship series as they dropped a decision to Neosho's Nighthawks before winning the next two games to capture that series three games to one.

Before the best of seven final series began, Fayetteville encountered a significant problem. It was announced that manager and regular catcher, Ken Blackman, would be unable to participate in the series due to a teaching commitment in Oxford Junction, Iowa. Pitcher

Andy Sinay was drafted for managerial duties, but the search for a competent catcher was more difficult.

Other league catchers like Melvin Autry of Monett and Al Harvatin of Siloam Springs had already left for their homes in Mississippi and Iowa, respectively, and attempts to re-sign ex-Fayetteville catcher Paul Rucker were unsuccessful. Finally, the Angels found a fellow named Carl Porter from somewhere and all was set for the Rogers face off.

Rogers won the first game at home on Saturday, September 4, as Lions pitcher Walter Nelson pitched a two-hitter in out-dueling Kenyon "Red" Cross who pitched a three-hitter himself. After the first game, rain played havoc with the rest of the series.

Paul Rucker
Photo courtesy of University of Arkansas Razorback Annual

Sunday's game scheduled for the Fair Grounds was rained out and Monday's game was moved to Rogers because of continued rain in Fayetteville. The move didn't seem to bother the Angels, though, as they beat Rogers to tie the series at one game apiece.

On Tuesday, September 7, the series returned to Fayetteville, but 1,250 disappointed fans saw Rogers defeat the local club. Wednesday and Thursday games were also washed out and the rains seemed to dampen Fayetteville's bats as well. On Friday, September 10, the Angels failed to score in dropping a 5-0 decision to the Lions, again in front of 1,250 home fans.

With Fayetteville trailing in the series three games to one, the fifth game was moved back to Rogers. Closing out both the Angels and the season, on Sunday, September 12, Rogers won 5-4 to take the series four games to one.

It was Rogers' third championship in the four years of the league's existence and brought the 1937 season—the most successful in Fayetteville franchise history, despite the championship series loss—to a close.

SIX
1938: Hitting on All Six, Mostly

TOWARD THE END of October 1937, Arkansas-Missouri League officials moved to fill the empty sixth slot in the league caused by the withdrawal of Vinita, Oklahoma, on the day before the 1937 season opened. The city that officials wooed and won ended up being Carthage, Missouri.

Carthage, which promised to provide a fine ballpark and a solid, supportive fan base, would also give the league a regional symmetry of three Arkansas and three Missouri clubs. By the end of the month Carthage was not only considered locked up as the new franchise but they had already been selected as a farm club by the Pittsburgh Pirates as well.

On January 30, 1938, the league held its annual mid-winter meeting at the Mountain Inn in Fayetteville. Bernal Seamster of Fayetteville was re-elected president of the league, Robert Henry of Siloam Springs was chosen to replace Rogers' J. O. Clark as VP, and Jim Bohart of Fayetteville was returned as secretary. Henry and Bill Cain, president of the Angels franchise, had recently been featured as outstanding minor league executives by *The Sporting News,* baseball's most prestigious periodical.

The biggest news of the 1938 preseason, however, was a monumental ruling handed down by the tough commissioner of baseball Judge Kennesaw Mountain Landis. In the early 1930s, Branch Rickey of the St. Louis Cardinals had conceived and put into place what is now known as the farm system whereby major league clubs own and operate, or sponsor, minor league teams in order to develop young ballplayers into big leaguers.

Judge Kennesaw Mountain Landis
Photo courtesy of Library of Congress

Before the 1935 season, Judge Landis had ruled that no major league club could operate more than one team in any minor league (the St. Louis Cardinals operated the entire Arkansas State League that season, but Landis' decision came after the local arrangement had been made).

Then in mid-March 1938, Landis' probe of the Cardinals system (Fayetteville's Fred Hawn was called to Chicago to testify in the inquiry) ended with a bombshell verdict. Though not generally known, this verdict had a direct, profound affect on the Arkansas-Missouri League and on Fayetteville's obscure Class D franchise.

After the Landis ruling, which was a direct assault on the minor league farm system in general and that of the St. Louis Cardinals in particular, the Arkansas-Missouri League was miraculously still standing. Landis fined a number of Cardinals farm teams (including Springfield, Missouri, Sacramento, California, and Cedar Rapids, Iowa) anywhere from $588 to $1,000 per club. He also declared free agents of some ninety-one ballplayers on contract with these franchises, including every player on the Monett, Missouri team of the Arkansas-Missouri League.

What this meant was that the "freed" players could sign with any team that wanted them. The impact on current and former Fayetteville players also was enormous as the ruling liberated well over a dozen—most now being with Cedar Rapids, the team that had sponsored the Angels (but no longer after the Landis ruling) during 1936 and 1937.[27]

As for the Arkansas-Missouri League itself, it would go on despite the Landis decision and it would have its usual 120-game schedule, this year opening May 7 and closing September 4 with both a regular season and a playoff champion crowned. An All-Star game was planned for July 11 between the league leader at that time against a group of all-stars selected from the other five clubs.

By the end of March 1938 then, and despite the Landis turmoil, the league was moving ahead at full speed. Managers and major league affiliations had been set for all clubs except Fayetteville, which had a new manager but no sponsor as yet.

TEAM	NICKNAME	MANAGER	SPONSOR
Fayetteville	Angels	Clifford "Bud" Knox	None, but hopeful
Siloam Springs	Travelers	Vincent "Moon" Mullen	St. Louis Browns
Neosho	Yankees	Denny Burns	New York Yankees
Rogers	Reds	Pat Patterson	Cincinnati Reds
Carthage	Pirates	Adolph "Buzz" Arlitt	Pittsburgh Pirates
Monett	Red Birds	Heinie Mueller	St. Louis Cardinals

In Fayetteville, Clifford "Bud" Knox, a man with a solid baseball pedigree, had been chosen manager. The Oskaloosa, Iowa native had played several years in the Southern Association and even briefly made it to the big leagues, playing a while for the Pittsburgh Pirates. In 1936 and 1937 he had played and managed at Mitchell of the Nebraska State League, leading that club to consecutive second place finishes and hitting a robust .347 in 1936.

Like his predecessors, Knox had to quickly put together a team and find a higher level club as a sponsor. In early April he and other Fayetteville officials met with New York Giants farm director Hank Deberry in Ft. Smith to discuss possible sponsorship by the major league club—it was not to be this year, however—and to look for playing talent.

A few days before spring training was to begin on April 18, Knox made what was by then an annual rite for Fayetteville managers: a trip to the Cardinals minor league camp in Springfield, Missouri to see what players could be picked up there.

When spring training did begin, around forty ballplayers made it to the Fair Grounds for the preseason workouts. Among those reporting were returnees Earl Naylor and Hugh Ward as well as free agents Earl "Inky" Watkins and Marv "Wimpy" Wolverton.

In typical Fayetteville fashion, bad April weather was a "bugaboo" for practicing and several sessions were canceled or curtailed. Still, towards the end of the month, the Angels played their first exhibition game, a win over Siloam Springs in front of 400 loyal Fair Grounds fans.

By May 3, when Knox had cut his squad to twenty players—two above the early season limit—the Angels had won an exhibition game against Ponca City (which once again provided hand-me-down uniforms to the Angels[28]), lost one to Rogers and beaten Siloam Springs. On May 4, the *Northwest Arkansas Times* carried its usual season opener ads, which included this year's list of "firsts" prizes for Angels ballplayers.

There was a touch of post-prohibition rowdiness about the prizes offered this season as the Smoke Shop—foregoing the usual awards of cake, Cokes, and cigarettes—offered a free bottle of beer to the first Angel who dropped by their business after the opening game.

The Smoke Shop, which was housed in the Palace Theatre building on the square, additionally offered a case of beer to the first Angel who hit a home run at the Fair Grounds and another case of beer to the team after they won their first home game. They also promised "$1 in trade" to the first Angel who "for any reason" was "kicked out" of a game. Fortunately for the tranquility of the team—and town—other merchants stayed with more traditional non-alcoholic prizes.[29]

All was then set for Fayetteville to open the 1938 Arkansas-Missouri League season, its fifth, on Saturday, May 7, against long time rival Siloam Springs. A ticket was still 35¢ for men, 25¢ for women and a dime for kids. The *Times* celebrated the opening game with a front-page headline and tentative starters were listed on the sports page.

Naturally, after the big buildup, the game was called because of wet grounds. The only game played opening day was at Monett where the Red Birds were beaten by the Carthage Pirates. An interesting sidelight to this game was that Monett featured shortstop Irwin Knoblauch while Carthage had Ed Knoblauch in right field and Charlie "Chuck" Knoblauch—uncle and namesake of recent big league player Chuck Knoblauch—at second base.

Fayetteville finally opened the season Sunday, May 8, with a road win over Siloam Springs. The next day the Angels defeated Monett in the home opener in front of 400 fans at the Fair Grounds. The Fayetteville starting lineup that day was:

Melvin Madden	3B
Tony Kruczyk	LF
Walt Nowak	RF
Earl Naylor	CF
Bill Seal	SS
Bud Knox	C
Melvin Schwab	1B
Glen Richardson	2B
Ralph Harris	P

Through the first two weeks of the season the Angels were a team of streaks, and only streaks. They opened league play with four straight wins, the last a victory over Carthage on May 11 in front of, again, 400 fans at the Fair Grounds. The Missouri club opened the season with all road games while they awaited the scheduled opening of their $40,000 park and lighting system.

After the Carthage win, Fayetteville lost three straight games but then won five in a row to take a half-game lead over Neosho for first place in the league. The second Angels victory in the win streak, in eleven innings over Siloam Springs at the Fair Grounds, came on the same day (May 17) that Carthage had their first home game in the new stadium, a dramatic come-from-behind victory over Monett before some 2,500 Carthaginians.

For the rest of the month the Angels were still a bit streaky, winning two games then losing three in going 4-5 during the next nine contests. They were doing much better than Siloam Springs, however, as the Travelers opened the season 0-9 before beating Monett to get in the win column.

On the last Sunday of May, Fayetteville and Siloam Springs split a double-header (both games were seven-inning affairs) with the Travelers winning the first and the Angels taking the second. In the double-header, the two teams set an Arkansas-Missouri League record by hitting ten home runs between them—four in the first game and six in the nightcap.

Fayetteville started June with a 2-3 record before small crowds as there was a "continuance of the worst baseball weather in the history of the Ark-Mo Loop." On Saturday, June 4, Monett drubbed the Angels at the Fair Grounds as the home club left the bases loaded four times and seventeen men on base in total to set a new league record.

That same day, Neosho set another league record, albeit a more positive one from a baseball standpoint, by stealing fifteen bases against the Rogers Reds. On June 10, Ed Smith of the Yankees got into the record books when he struck out seventeen Siloam Springs Travelers in a win at Neosho.

Irwin Knoblauch
Photo courtesy of Powers Museum, Carthage, Missouri

After their mini-slump, the Angels notched another five game win skein to move into a virtual tie with Carthage for first place on June 13. Fayetteville had two more wins than Carthage at this point but also two more losses and therefore statistically they trailed the Pirates by percentage points. It was still the latest in the season Fayetteville had been this close to the top in franchise history.

Three of the wins were over Rogers as Angels' pitcher Rudy Heyne continued his mastery of the Reds with a two-hit win on June 8. At that point, Heyne had pitched twenty-seven innings against Rogers without giving up a single earned run. Fayetteville was so good on the road, in fact, that during the first month of the season they compiled a 13-2 record away from their own ballpark.

The Angels stayed around the top of the league standings even though they were 3-2 for their next five games. On June 11, they lost at Monett while Neosho was winning at Siloam Springs in a game called after seven innings because all nine of the official baseballs were all "used up."

Fayetteville won their next three, then lost to Siloam Springs—who "improved" their record to 4-26. On June 14, the *Times* declared in a stacked headline: "Fayetteville Playing Best Winning Baseball in History," and despite the loss to Siloam Springs that evening, the team went out and proved the paper right by winning six in a row.

The Angels' winning streak began June 15 with a victory at Siloam Springs, where veteran baseball man, Runt Marr, had just been hired by club president Robert Henry, to replace Moon Mullen at the helm of the struggling Travelers squad. On June 17 ex-Angel Doug White re-signed with the club after being cut by Cedar Rapids. He promptly proceeded to knock in the tying and winning runs in a victory at Carthage.[30]

The team kept on winning, beating Carthage again, then Neosho, and Rogers twice before Neosho halted the string by defeating the Angels June 22 at the Fair Grounds—the same night as Joe Louis' historic one-round knockout of Max Schmeling, the pride of Nazi Germany.

Fayetteville's winning streak had put them back into first place in the league, but they then lost three in a row (all to Neosho) and five of eight overall to finish the month on a slightly down note but still solidly in second place. In a 13-5 loss to Neosho on June 23, Fayetteville made an astonishing nine errors which would have set an all-time league record except that Siloam Springs eclipsed that mark the very same day by making ten errors themselves in a game against Carthage. In another record-setting performance, Carthage left-handed pitcher, Leon Skidgel, struck out 18 Neosho Yankees on June 20 to establish a new all-time league mark.

June ended with a loss to Monett—which now featured major leaguer-to-be Erv Dusak—but Fayetteville returned the favor the following night, July 1, beating the Red Birds in the first ever night game at Monett. Angels' third baseman, Hans "Whitey" Kreuger, tied "Doc" Ledbetter's all-time single-game league record by getting six hits in six times at bat.

The win put Fayetteville back into first place, yet another team record for leading the league this far into a season. Over the long Fourth of July weekend, however, the bottom fell out for the Angels. They lost three straight, giving up 32 runs in losing to Neosho and Rogers (twice). Walter Lemke reported that, in their last six games, Angels pitchers had allowed an extraordinary 88 hits and 65 runs.[31]

The losing streak dropped Fayetteville to third place behind Carthage and Neosho. After beating Rogers on the road July 5, the Angels were defeated twice in a row including a loss to Rogers on Ladies' Night, July 6, at the Fair Grounds in front of 750 fans, the "largest crowd of the year."

On Thursday, July 7, the mid-season league All-Stars were announced. President Bernal Seamster had decided to have the All-Star game be a battle between Arkansas and Missouri players and it was scheduled for July 11 in Carthage.

Fayetteville placed seven men on the Arkansas squad including Rudy Heyne (Pitcher), Harry Williams (Pitcher), Bill Seal (Infielder), Earl Naylor (Outfielder), Robert David and Whitey Kreuger (both utility players), and Bud Knox, who would manage the Arkansas All-Stars. Sherm Lollar, later a major league all-star and the namesake of the Fayetteville Little League in the mid-1950s, was named batboy for the Arkansans.

The much-honored Angels responded by winning three in a row leading up to the All-Star break. On Friday, July 8, they beat Carthage at the Fair Grounds despite a home run by Carthage manager, Buzz Arlitt, who the *Times* reported, a la Babe Ruth, pointed to where he would hit the ball and then did just that.

That same night, Neosho beat Siloam Springs for the Yankees' tenth straight win, and Monett roughed-up Rogers at home in front of several big league scouts and Mr. St. Louis Cardinals himself, Branch Rickey. The next night Monett's Kenneth Rutledge broke the all-time Arkansas-Missouri League strikeout record (the third time it had been broken during the season) by fanning 20 Carthage Pirates in a 2-0 Monett win at Carthage.

League standings at the break were as follows:

Arkansas-Missouri League
(Standings at All-Star Break)

Team	Won	Lost	Pct
Neosho	37	22	.627
Carthage	38	24	.613
Fayetteville	38	24	.613
Rogers	31	30	.508
Monett	25	36	.410
Siloam Springs	12	45	.211

Missouri won the battle of the state All-Stars Monday night, July 11, in Carthage with a 4-2 decision in front of 3,000 fans in a game highlighted by a pair of two-run home runs by Neosho's base-stealing flash, Steve Luby, and Carthage's Ray Lawrence. Fayetteville's Bill Seal got the only extra base hit for Arkansas, a triple in the top of the seventh inning.

Fayetteville started play after the All-Star break tied with Carthage for second place just one and one-half games behind front running Neosho, but then the Angels lost three in a row. They first lost to Siloam Springs on the road in twelve innings. Neosho then beat the Angels two straight with Yankees speedster, Steve Luby, homering both nights.

Now alone in third place, Fayetteville finished the month of July poorly—going 5-9, including loss streaks of three and four games. In Rogers, Cyril "Butch" Moran, Reds first baseman, went on a hitting tear and broke ex-Fayetteville star Pete Ashmore's consecutive hit streak (eight) by connecting for nine straight hits over a three-game span. Moran's batting heroics helped Rogers win thirteen of sixteen games through the middle of the month.

Roman Deller, stellar pitcher for Carthage, hurled two complete seven-inning victories in the Pirates' home double-header sweep of Siloam Springs on July 18. Fayetteville's Earl Naylor joined the record setters on July 19 by making eight putouts in the field (the second time he'd done that during the season) and then threw out a base runner to add an assist to his total which gave Naylor the league record for chances by an outfielder in a regulation game with nine.

While the Angels struggled along, Carthage and Neosho played leapfrog for first place with Neosho being the better leaper most of the time. In other league news, Hershel Morris of Monett tied a league record July 24 by hitting a home run in three consecutive at bats against Siloam Springs, which had released him earlier in the season. Despite all the homers, Monett manager Heinie Mueller was let go July 26 and replaced by old time major leaguer Frank Sigafoos. Mueller was given a travel bag as a goodbye gift by the Monett fans.

During Fayetteville's four-game losing streak late in the month, Neosho beat them twice, in eleven innings at the Fair Grounds on July 27 and in a regulation nine-innings the next night in Carthage. In the first game, Carthage stole two bases to bring their league-leading and record-setting total to 219 stolen bases ("100 more than their nearest rival") in only 73 games. In the second contest, Carthage pitcher Bill Gill handed Fayetteville their first shutout loss of the year and struck out nineteen batters in the process.

At Siloam Springs, the Travelers managed a three-game winning streak, their longest of the year, and in Monett on July 30, Neosho beat the Red Birds 19-1 in a contest called off after seven innings by the rival managers when it became obvious that Monett simply couldn't get anybody out. Fayetteville, meanwhile, closed the month with two wins to nest solidly in third place, seven games back of standings-topper Neosho.

The August 1 game at the Fair Grounds was a memorable one. Fayetteville was beaten 5-2 by Neosho, which was not so memorable, but probably the largest crowd ever to see a professional minor league contest in town—2,500 strong—thronged the stands free of charge on "Friends of Congressman Claude A. Fuller Night."

An August 5 game was moved to Rogers where 2,000 watched Carthage beat the Angels in a seven-inning contest also paid for by the Fuller "Friends." Mr. Fuller completed his "baseball" campaign by sponsoring a game at Siloam Springs on August 8, which Neosho won from the homestanding Travelers.[32]

After the loss to Neosho on Claude Fuller Night, Fayetteville lost three more in a row before beating Carthage twice on August 3 and 4. The bright spot for the Angels was second baseman Bill Seal who hit

Howard "Chick" Wagenhurst
Photo courtesy of Powers Museum, Carthage, Missouri

home runs in three straight games over two days, each time with first baseman Melvin Schwab on base.

In Monett, the Red Birds were falling apart. They lost eight in a row, won two, then lost four in a row, but at least when they played Siloam Springs it wasn't hitting that kept these two bottom rung teams down.

On August 1 Siloam Springs won 18-13 at Monett, the two teams combining for thirty-four hits between them. Then on August 4, also at Monett, Siloam Springs won 26-16 with the clubs hacking out a total of 36 hits. Another big offensive display occurred in the league on August 11 when Neosho scored seventeen runs in the seventh inning of a 20-12 home win over Carthage.

Breaking out of their early August doldrums, Fayetteville went 7-3 over a ten game stretch to fend off a Rogers run and remain securely in third place as of August 17. On a very windy Sunday, August 14, the Angels swept lowly Monett 12-8 and 20-4 (the second game was called after five and one-half innings) at the Fair Grounds.

The old "spheroid" (as the narrator of "Casey at the Bat" might say) really flew that day as the two teams hit a total of thirteen home runs, ten by Fayetteville. The first five batters in the Angels lineup each had two home runs in the double-header. In the first game, Paul Young hit both of his home runs in successive at bats, a feat duplicated by Earl Naylor in the second contest.

On August 15, Fayetteville got eighteen hits in a win at Siloam Springs as three players (Whitey Kreuger, Melvin Schwab, and Inky Watkins) each had four hits in the game. Also that day, Monett's elderly manager Frank Sigafoos hit two home runs in a loss at Neosho while, over in Carthage, Pirates pitchers Howard "Chick" Wagenhurst and Leon Skidgel combined for a nine-inning 7-0 no-hit win over Rogers.

For the rest of the month, however, and even though they did have a five-game winning streak, the Angels played just better than .500 ball going 9-8 through August 31. Despite the overall mediocrity, there was some exciting on-field action as Fayetteville scored twelve runs in the fourth inning of a 15-7 win over Carthage at home August 21, a game in which Carthage manager Buzz Arlitt, always the clown, crawled and slid into home while scoring one of the Pirates' runs that day.

Other league news at this time was made off the playing field. On August 18 it was reported that Runt Marr, manager of 30-65 Siloam Springs, had relinquished his job to catcher Mike Sertich and in Fayetteville on August 20, club business manager V. James Ptak announced that home paid attendance in July and August was very poor and had in fact dropped 50% from 1937 levels.[33]

On August 24, another peculiar off-field incident occurred when the Neosho Yankees bus broke down on their way home from a loss at Fayetteville. A local farmer, thinking the traveling group of athletes were "bandits," took two shots at the players—luckily not hitting any of them. Then August 31, Fayetteville's bus also broke down (coming back from a loss at Carthage) and while the team wasn't shot at, it did take three more buses to get the team home early the next morning as two of the replacement buses stopped running as well.

In yet another strange, and not funny, incident, Harry Williams—a fine pitcher for Fayetteville—had his pitching arm shot and broken Friday night, August 26, by a man named Ed Clark, whose niece Williams was dating. Clark testified that he thought Williams was a "chicken thief" and fired three shots at the ballplayer. One round hit Williams' right arm, effectively ending the young pitcher's career.

On the ballfields, Roman Deller, the Carthage iron man pitcher, did it again—pitching two complete seven-inning victories against Fayetteville on August 22. Just four days earlier Deller had beaten Neosho in front of a Merchant's Night crowd of 4,000 in Carthage.

At Neosho on August 23, the flying Yankees stole eight bases against Fayetteville catcher Inky Watkins in a Neosho win. For the sake of tradition it would seem, "Hornbuckle" Buck Buchanan showed up again and, in a relief role, got the next to last win in Fayetteville's five-game win streak, a decision over Monett at the Fair Grounds.

At the start of September, Fayetteville won three straight—beating Rogers on Fan Appreciation Night (all the players and batboy Lollar received crisp new five dollar bills); then defeating Siloam Springs to clinch third place (Neosho captured the regular season pennant the same day); and finally besting Monett in eleven innings (Whitey Kreuger, Angels third baseman, played every position except catcher). The team ended the season on September 4 with a loss to champion Neosho in a game played in front of 400 spectators in Joplin, Missouri.

The final standings for 1938 were as follows:

Arkansas-Missouri League
(Final Standings)

Team	Won	Lost	Pct
Neosho	73	42	.635
Carthage	69	49	.585
Fayetteville	66	53	.555
Rogers	63	54	.538
Monett	44	74	.373
Siloam Springs	36	79	.313

The two best three out of five semifinal playoff series, matching Neosho against Rogers and Carthage against Fayetteville, began on Tuesday, September 6. Rogers lost at Neosho and Fayetteville lost to Carthage before a crowd of 500 to 600 fans at the Fair Grounds. Because of continuing low attendance, Fayetteville club president Bill Cain announced that the rest of the series would be played in Carthage where the Pirates usually drew from 1,200 to 2,000 paying customers per game.

The change of venue seemed to help the Angels as they won two of three at Carthage. Neosho, meanwhile, beat Rogers twice more to sweep that series three games to none. Fayetteville and Carthage, tied at 2 wins apiece, would battle in a fifth and final game for the right to play Neosho for the league championship.

Due to surprisingly small crowds at Carthage—the largest reported attendance was about 500—the fifth and deciding game between the Angels and Pirates was shifted back to Fayetteville. There, on Sunday, September 11, 850 fans (the largest Fair Grounds crowd of the playoffs) watched Carthage beat the Angels and take the series with a tight 6-5 win. Jim Bohart of the *Times* described it as "probably the most exciting game ever played at the Fair Grounds" as a late two-run rally in the bottom of the ninth inning fell one run short for the Angels.

Before that final Fayetteville-Carthage game, yet another tragedy befell a former player in the league. Maurice "Babe" Chartrand, who had pitched for both Fayetteville and Monett during the 1937 season, and who had been playing for Beatrice in the Nebraska State League, died Friday, September 9, of complications following an operation for a leg infection.

On a less somber note, the final playoff series between Neosho and Carthage was a short affair. Carthage overpowered the regular season champions (Neosho could only manage a win at home on September 15) to take the playoff title four games to one. With crowds averaging around 1,000 or more per contest, the first All-Missouri Arkansas-Missouri League championship playoff series put a final punctuation mark to what was, overall, probably the league's most successful and well-attended season.

SEVEN
1939: Regular Season Champs

DESPITE FIELDING THE most competitive team in its five-year history and making the playoffs for the second straight year, the Fayetteville franchise was where it always seemed to be in the off-season—and during the regular season for that matter—looking for a way to keep itself afloat economically. The Angels played 1938 without a sponsor and attendance at the Fair Grounds had dropped from a peak of 19,950 in 1937 to just 13,850 in 1938. The club was $650 in debt and in danger of not being able to answer the bell for the upcoming 1939 season.

On the other hand, the Missouri clubs—Carthage, Monett, and Neosho—were set for 1939. Neosho had been given permission by the league to transfer to Pittsburg, Kansas but that move proved unnecessary and by late November 1938 all three teams already had big league sponsors.

For original league members Siloam Springs and Rogers, however, prospects for 1939 looked slim. Neither club had sponsors and neither could survive without the extra financial aid. The league's decision to raise the total monthly salary limit to $1,000, exclusive of managers, only made things more difficult for the struggling clubs.

The front-page headline of the *Northwest Arkansas Times* for Friday, December 30, 1938 declared "1939 To Be A Year of Prosperity." The optimism of that headline was borne out on the baseball front less than a month later when the *Times* reported on January 23, 1939 that Fayetteville's Angels had found a sponsor—the lowly, but to local officials franchise-saving, St. Louis Browns.

At a meeting of Fayetteville officials, fans, and interested parties exactly one week later, V. James Ptak—pinch hitting for club president W. A. "Bill" Cain—told the assemblage that the Browns would loan Fayetteville $600 to pay last year's debts and also provide "$1,800 [in] financial aid during the season" in exchange for the rights to all players on the team.

To show the big league club that Fayetteville was solidly behind the Angels and approved of the new sponsorship, Ptak also suggested that letters of appreciation—"especially from business concerns and civic organizations"—be sent to the Browns' St. Louis office.

The Arkansas-Missouri League held its annual winter meeting Sunday, February 5, at the Mountain Inn in Fayetteville. Once more, there would be a 120-game schedule, with opening day set for April 28, and the league was assured of at least four clubs for 1939. Siloam Springs and Rogers, the two wavering franchises, were given until February 20 (later extended to March 6) to rejoin Fayetteville, Carthage, Monett, and Neosho in the Arkansas-Missouri League.

On March 7, 1939 Fayetteville club president Bill Cain announced that a 24-year-old up-and-coming Brown's farmhand, second baseman Frank Oceak, would take the managerial reins for this year's edition of the Angels.

A fine player in his own right, Oceak—who would have a long career as a major league coach—brought an enthusiasm and fire with him never before seen in Fayetteville. The Cliffside Park, New Jersey, native had broken into professional baseball in 1933 and in his first year as a player-manager had guided Lafayette, Louisiana, of the class D Evangeline League, to a fifth place finish in 1938.

In other notable off-season news, Fayetteville's Bernal Seamster, citing business reasons, resigned as president of the Arkansas-Missouri League after a three-year stint at the top. League officials meeting in Neosho voted in veteran Siloam Springs baseball man Robert Henry as the new president.

J. O. Clark of Rogers was named vice-president and Jim Bohart of Fayetteville was re-elected secretary. Henry would also double as league treasurer. On March 24, the *Times* reported that Fayetteville native and local favorite, Fred Hawn, would return to the league as manager of the Monett Red Birds.

Spring training was scheduled to begin Tuesday, April 18 and what was hoped to be "Fayetteville's best baseball club" was starting to take shape. New manager Oceak soon brought the nucleus of the team with him, but several former local and league players, including Rudy Heyne, C. J. Odneal, Clifford Stebe, and Harry Williams—making an aborted comeback attempt after a gunshot accident late in the 1938 season—were also on hand for early workouts.

On Sunday, April 16, Oceak and several players arrived in Fayetteville from the Browns camp in Mayfield, Kentucky, ready for the scheduled opening of baseball drills that following Tuesday. Oceak decided to begin training a day early on Monday and although some twenty-five hopefuls were on hand to start the daily 10 a.m. to 4 p.m. practice sessions at the Fair Grounds, the pre-emptive first session was called off due to wet grounds.

Spring training did get started as scheduled the next day and, although poor weather would hamper the early workouts as it frequently had in past seasons, it was soon evident to careful observers that this was not going to be one of your Fayetteville teams from the past.

The team's first exhibition game—against a group of University of Arkansas and local all-stars, including former Fayetteville players Doug White, Cline Watson, and Buck Buchanan, as well as local star athlete Buster Dunlap—was held Saturday, April 22. The new deal Angels, led by Ken Grosse and Rudy Briner destroyed the All-Stars 22-0. The next day the Angels pounded an independent club, the Choteau, Oklahoma (hometown of Fayetteville pitcher C. J. Odneal) Cowboys, 18-6.

The season opener at Carthage on April 28 was less than a week away and the Angels hustled through spring training as best they could—allowing for more weather interference. Leading up to Day One, the *Times* began running a series of player profiles called "Meet the Angels." The short bios, giving hometowns, nicknames, positions, and the like, introduced the new players to local fans. It was a nice touch and was inaugurated with profiles of Clarence "Ripper" or "Rip" Collins, utility man and third baseman Harry Hatch.

1939 had been determined to be (or perhaps selected as) the one-hundredth anniversary of baseball in the United States and, accordingly, on Saturday, April 29, the *Times* ran an exciting ad for the start of the new season. The Arkansas-Missouri League would return to a split season schedule this year after abandoning the format during the 1937 and 1938 seasons, and the first and second-half winners would meet for the playoff title.

As they often had in the past, Fayetteville lost the season opener, this time in Carthage 2-1 before 1,000 fans in what the *Times* said was "one of the best early season pitching duels ever seen" in the Arkansas-Missouri League. Over in Neosho, in the other opening day battle, Monett defeated the Yankees 3-1. The most exciting event of opening day did not, however, occur on the ball fields.

While Arkansas-Missouri League president Robert Henry, of Siloam Springs, and some friends were playing good Samaritans by driving two umpires up to the Carthage-Fayetteville season opening game Friday night, April 28, unknown to them there had been a jail break in Neosho and they, the Henry party, fit the description of the criminals.

Hauled in by authorities in Carthage, Henry and the others were fortunate that the local jailer—a man named Ora Six—recognized the Arkansas-Missouri League president and the group was released in time for the Fayetteville-Carthage game to go on as scheduled. "Umpires usually have their troubles after the game," quipped Henry, "not before."

Back on the ballfields and sandwiched around the opening day loss at Carthage and a May 2 defeat at Neosho, Fayetteville's new breed of Angels put together two three-game winning streaks. They beat Carthage 1-0 in the home opener at the Fair Grounds Saturday night, April 29, behind, ace pitcher, George Bender's two-hitter. Bender pitched no-hit ball for seven and two-thirds innings and drove in the game's only run for good measure.

The next afternoon, dressed in their new white uniforms (they had worn gray ones on opening night), the Angels again beat the Pirates at the Fair Grounds. Spirited manager Oceak drove in three runs with a bases-loaded double then got into a fight with Carthage outfielder Harvey Beaster. Both players were ejected from the game.

Fayetteville's starting lineup (excluding pitchers Bender and Mike Barbolla—Sunday's winning pitcher) was the same for both games:

Ken Grosse	1B
Paul Young	LF
Joe Szuch	RF
Rudy Briner	C
Frank Oceak	2B
Norm Litzinger	CF
Ed Checkley	SS
Harry Hatch	3B

Tuesday, May 2, 1939, was a day that would resonate down through time and forever affect anyone who has followed baseball through the years. On that far away day, Lou Gehrig—the "Iron Horse"—removed himself from the New York Yankees lineup after having played in 2,130 consecutive games—a record that lasted almost sixty years and that inspired countless players and non-players alike through the ages.

Gehrig pulled himself because he felt, that with his poor performance of late, "it might help the club" if he didn't play. The once great Yankee's days as a player were over, and in less than two years, he was dead from amyotrophic lateral sclerosis, the illness which now bears the great slugger's name.

That same Tuesday evening Fayetteville lost at Neosho but returned the favor the next day by beating the Yankees at the Fair Grounds. They then defeated Monett, also at home, before 800 fans on 10¢ game night, and followed with another win, defeating the Red Birds in Monett on May 5.

At that point, the Angels were 6-2 on the young year and in first place by two games, not a place that previous Fayetteville teams had been used to occupying. Yet during the next ten days they played even better, losing at Monett on May 6, but then reeling off seven straight wins.

On Sunday, May 7, the Angels beat Neosho twice in games moved to the Fair Grounds because Neosho wasn't allowed to play Sunday games in their ballpark. In the second game, a young catcher from Neosho knocked out a solo home run in his team's defeat. His name was Ralph Houk and, although he would have the bad luck of becoming the backup to New York Yankees Hall of Fame catcher Yogi Berra, the Neosho backstop would go on to have an eight-year career as a major league player and a twenty-year career as a big league manager, winning pennants with the Yankees in 1961, 1962, and 1963.[34]

Fayetteville, meanwhile, kept winning. They released hard luck pitcher Harry Williams but then beat Carthage on the road and again back at the Fair Grounds. Rain forced several cancellations in mid-May, but when the Angels played they won: twice over Neosho at the Fair Grounds, May 14; and then over Monett on Ladies' Night, May 15, before a crowd of 850, four hundred of whom were ladies. The Monett win was the Angels' tenth consecutive home win, and at this point, they were remarkably, even amazingly, undefeated at home for the year.

The Angels were playing so well that Walter Lemke told the readers of his "Angel Food" column in the *Times* that this was "the best team that has ever represented Fayetteville" in the history of the league. Lemke's early judgement would end up being not only prophetic but flatly true as well.

Elsewhere in the league, in a double-header, May 14, Carthage manager/first baseman Buzz Arlitt tied the league record by hitting four consecutive home runs against Monett. Arlitt hit a two-run game-winning home run to win the first half of a doubleheader, then hit home runs in the second, fourth, and fifth innings of the second game, also a Carthage victory.

In Fayetteville, the Angels kept winning. For the first week past

Walter J. Lemke
Photo courtesy of University of Arkansas Special Collections Loc. 268

mid-May they were 5-2 including their twelfth straight home win. On May 23, they were seven games ahead of second place Carthage and still sitting in the catbird seat. Club officials, buoyed by the team's performance, started a special "Booster" ticket drive (for 50¢ a fan got a ticket and a chance for prizes or reduced rates on future games) "to make at least 2,500 persons in the city and vicinity 'baseball conscious'."

On Thursday, May 25, the Angels players were special guests of the Rotary Club for a luncheon at the Mountain Inn. Fayetteville team president Bill Cain, in introducing the players, declared them to be "the best bunch of boys I ever worked with" and the kind of fellows who "seem always to do the right thing at the right time." Spliced around all the praise and excitement and several rainouts, the Angels beat Neosho on another Ladies Night at the Fair Grounds and then bested Monett at the Missourian's field.

On Saturday, May 27, after a series of rained-out games, Fayetteville's home unbeaten streak ended at twelve when Monett beat the Angels at the Fair Grounds. The loss triggered a mini-collapse and the Angels lost five in a row before righting the ship with a home victory over Monett on May 31.

During the bad streak, league president Henry fined Fayetteville manager Frank Oceak $10 for a "run-in" the Angels leader had with umpires during the second game of a May 28 double-header in which Fayetteville lost both games to Carthage. Despite the losses, the Angels still ended the month with a four-game lead over Neosho.

During the first ten days of June, Fayetteville again played well going 6-3. Among the highlights were victories at Carthage on June 4 and another over Neosho at the Fair Grounds June 6. In the latter game, the Angels overcame a seven-error performance and a five-run deficit by scoring eight runs in the bottom of the eighth inning as they—in Walter Lemke's words—"smote the foreign invader from Missouri."

Angels pitcher Ed Smith added more personal highlights among those of the team as he won decisions on June 4, 5, 7, and 9—giving him league records for wins at three in four days and then four wins in six days to bring his season record to 9-2.

Through mid-June, the Angels put together a four-game winning streak (starting with Smith's fourth straight pitching victory) and after the games of June 15 were seven games ahead of second place Carthage. The league was having some unusual contests about this time: Carthage and Monett pitchers walked 26 batters between them in a 12-6 Carthage home win on June 7; 3,000 Merchant's Night fans came out for a Neosho loss at Carthage on June 8; and Neosho defeated Carthage in a slugfest, 18-14, at Neosho on June 14.

Also on June 14, Fayetteville put on the biggest offensive show in Arkansas-Missouri League history. With Ken Grosse scoring a league

Charlie Knoblauch
Photo courtesy of Powers Museum, Carthage, Missouri

record six runs, Fayetteville had 25 hits in defeating the hapless Monett Red Birds 26-5 at the Fair Grounds.

In the next few days Fayetteville kept up its run-scoring barrage. They won four games in a row including 16-6 over Neosho in the seven-inning finale to a June 15 double-header in Missouri, and then overpowered Carthage the next day 21-2 to hand the Pirates their worst home (or road) loss in their two years in the league. Ken Grosse set another league record by getting a hit in four consecutive innings of the Carthage game (he had singles in the first, second, third, and fourth innings). All in all, Fayetteville scored 68 runs in just three days.

Sunday, June 18, the Angels won a double-header at Monett with pitcher Clifford Stebe getting the victory in both games (the second in relief). Ace pitcher George Bender ran his record to 10-1 with a home win over Monett June 20 and two days later Ed Smith pitched a complete game win over Carthage at the Fair Grounds to improve his record to 10-3. Smith's win allowed the Angels to clinch the first half-season pennant—the first championship of any kind for Fayetteville in their six years in the league.

The first half officially closed on June 27 with an Angels loss at Monett, but Fayetteville still ended up seven full games ahead of Carthage, their nearest rival. The standings were as follows:

Arkansas-Missouri League
(Final standings—first half)

Team	Won	Lost	Pct
Fayetteville	38	20	.655
Carthage	31	27	.555
Neosho	29	33	.468
Monett	21	39	.350

After an off day, the Angels played a group of Missouri players, including Carthage's Harvey Beaster and Bob Playfair and Neosho's Charlie Knoblauch and Ralph Houk (Monett had two players selected but they did not make it to the game), in an All-Star game held at the Fair Grounds on June 28. The fans showed up with 1,000 to 1,400 fans on hand to watch the team Jim Bohart described as "the best baseball club ever to represent" the city and "probably one of the best ever to perform in the Arkansas-Missouri League" defeat the Missourians 10-9 in ten innings.

When the second half of the season began the next day, June 30, Fayetteville lost their first game at Carthage, but won ten of their next eleven games through July 10. During the streak, they won three games in a row—including a one-hit, 2-0, win by "Big" George Bender over Monett on July 2. Bender faced only 28 Red Bird hitters, one over the

Carthage Pirates, 1939
Photo courtesy of John G. Hall

minimum, and raised his record to 12-1 but he did it in front of one of the "smallest crowds of the season" at the Fair Grounds—before suffering a single loss to Neosho.

After the loss, Fayetteville won seven games in a row, the first coming on the same day (July 5) it was reported that Charlie Barrett, well-known Cardinals scout and frequent visitor at Angels games, had died of a heart attack in St. Louis. Barrett had been in the stands in Fayetteville as recently as June 23.

On the playing field, the news was that Ken Grosse was on a record-breaking hitting streak. On July 6, Grosse went 4 for 5 in an Angels home win over Carthage, thus hitting safely in his twenty-third consecutive game. The Fayetteville first baseman kept going: twenty-four straight, twenty-five, and on. Finally, on July 10, Grosse was held hitless in an Angels win over Carthage at the Fair Grounds. Grosse's hitting streak was stopped at twenty-seven straight games, an all-time Arkansas-Missouri League record.

When the dust settled after Grosse's record-setting streak, Fayetteville was in first place, three games ahead of Neosho. George Bender had raised his record to 13-2 and on July 8 Bob Bennett hit for the cycle. Yet the home crowds were still small. President Cain reduced ticket prices (25¢ for men and 15¢ for women) and drew 700 fans on July 11 but attendance was still weak—especially considering how good this Angels club was.

The team seemed to react to the low attendance and they went through a rough spell on the field. They lost three in a row through July 13, then managed a home win over Carthage, but lost three of their next four. After losing at Carthage on Monday, July 17, the *Times* reported the next day that the Fayetteville club—due to poor crowds it was said—had failed to fully meet players' salaries on July 15.

Despite its off the field troubles, the team was still in first place. They lost a 4-0 decision to Neosho (the first time they'd been shut out all year) on Angels "Appreciation Night," July 19, but then won three in a row. Yet Walter Lemke, in his "Angel Food" column for July 21, had a dire prediction: "If attendance does not improve," he warned, "it looks as if Fayetteville's days in organized baseball are numbered."

The very next day president Bill Cain turned the Fayetteville franchise over to the league. Arkansas-Missouri League president Henry, hoping to salvage the season and the Fayetteville club, said that the team could stay in town "if the fans want to keep it."

"$600 Needed to Keep Baseball Club" read a huge *Northwest Arkansas Times* front-page headline on Wednesday, July 26, and the accompanying story detailed how the Chamber of Commerce, civic, and veterans groups had met to come up with a plan for saving the Angels franchise.

The plan was to hold a "Dollar Night" at the Fair Grounds. Admission would be $1 with all proceeds going to cover club expenses in order to keep the team in Fayetteville (Miami, Oklahoma, had shown some interest in taking over the franchise).

On Friday night, July 28, Dollar Night was held—Fayetteville, behind George Bender's fourteen strikeouts, beat Neosho—and $400 was raised. Although the sum was shy of the full amount needed, it was enough to save the team. On July 31, league president Henry thanked the civic groups and fans who, working together, had kept "organized baseball in Fayetteville."

Remarkably enough in this difficult time, the Angels managed to play very well. They had a five-game winning streak toward the end of July and finished the month by taking ten of thirteen games overall to maintain their hold on first place, two and one-half games ahead of Neosho. Along the way their offensive machine had kept up its torrid pace.

On July 21 the Angels won at Monett 17-13, defeated Neosho 19-8, the next day, then beat Monett again—this time at home—15-1 on July 25. They beat the Red Birds badly three more times: 15-7 and 10-5 there July 26 and 27, and 12-4 at the Fair Grounds July 30. Fayetteville put the wraps on July with a 12-9 home win over Carthage on the last day of the month.

In early August, however, the team only managed to tread water, playing .500 ball (3-3) for the first week. George Bender beat Neosho at the Fair Grounds August 4 to raise his league leading record to 17-3, but the Angels were just so-so overall. Then they did it again. They went on another winning streak, this time taking seven straight decisions.

They beat poor Monett in Fayetteville on August 7 as the hapless Red Birds left sixteen runners on base—one shy of the league record. The next night, also at home, Bender struck out thirteen in shutting out Carthage 6-0 to go 18-3 on the year. On August 9, the Angels again beat Monett in a game delayed an hour and a half because Fayetteville's bus broke down on the way to the Missouri town.

Friday night, August 11, was an exciting night for local fans. Not only did the Angels beat Neosho 12-5 (Fayetteville slammed out 19 hits) but the 600 customers at the Fair Grounds park got to see a pre-game track meet between the two teams.

Additionally, 400 of those folks came to the game on a 50¢ combination ticket plan cooked up by local theatre entrepreneur W. F. Sonneman to help himself and the baseball franchise. For the price of one ticket, fans got to see the Angels game and a Randolph Scott western, *The Frontier Marshall*, at the Ozark Theatre.

The seventh and last win in the Angels streak came in the second game of a double-header sweep of Neosho at the Fair Grounds August 13 and was punctuated by the sale of pitcher Clifford Stebe (who won his seventeenth game in the first half of the twin bill). Stebe was promoted to the parent St. Louis Browns' Youngstown club in the Class C Middle Atlantic League. The transaction gave the Fayetteville club a much-needed injection of $250 cash.

Fayetteville finally lost at Neosho on August 14 and manager Oceak was ejected for arguing an umpire's call at third base—the incident costing the skipper a fine and a suspension from league president Henry. Still, at mid-month, the Angels had a five game cushion between them and second place Neosho.

In the last two weeks of the season, Fayetteville played solid, if not spectacular, ball going 8-7 for their last fifteen contests. At a Thursday, August 17, loss to Carthage at the Fair Grounds, fans showed Frank Oceak their appreciation by raising $17.50 of the $25 fine imposed on the manager by league president Henry. Even more remarkably, Carthage fans raised the remaining $7.50 the following night when the Pirates beat the Angels at the Missouri team's park.

Thursday, August 24, was a big day for Fayetteville. Even though their scheduled double-header at Neosho was rained out, Fayetteville won the second half-season pennant when the last-place Monett Red Birds defeated Carthage at home.

"Angels Clinch Ark-Mo Full Season Championship" proudly proclaimed a huge banner headline on the *Times* sports page Friday, August 25.

Fayetteville's Angels had thus accomplished something no other Arkansas State/Arkansas-Missouri League team had ever done: win both titles in a split-season year. Happy fans could have celebrated the Angels' triumph that night by going to see popular western swing band Bob Wills and the Texas Playboys, who were playing at the National Guard Armory—admission 40¢.

On the last Saturday of the regular season, George Bender shut out Monett 8-0 at the Fair Grounds in upping his record to 20-4.

The victory made Bender the only twenty-game winner in the league for 1939.

In the next to last game, an Angels win at Monett, Clarence "Ripper" Collins pitched a five-hit complete game for the win and in doing so had, during the course of the full season, played every position in the field—a very rare accomplishment in professional baseball.

On Tuesday, August 29, Fayetteville ended their season with a home loss to Neosho. The night wasn't a complete loss, however, as fans presented manager Oceak with a new set of golf clubs, golf bag, and a dozen balls. Each player and batboy, Sherm Lollar, was presented with a tie.

The second-half final standings were as follows:

Arkansas-Missouri League
(Final standings—second half)

Team	Won	Lost	Pct
Fayetteville	41	22	.651
Carthage	36	27	.571
Neosho	36	28	.563
Monett	14	50	.219

Even though Fayetteville had won both halves of the regular season, league president Henry ruled there would still be a playoff series. Because Carthage had finished in second place, also during both halves of the season, the Pirates would meet the champion Angels in a best of seven series beginning August 30. Before the playoffs began, though, there was something of a controversy about the All-Star team that was announced August 28.

"Many Angels Overlooked In All-Star Vote" read a sports headline that day in the *Northwest Arkansas Times*. Fayetteville stars like Joe Szuch, Ken Grosse, and Harry Hatch (who had hit 50 points better than Grant Harris of Carthage the player selected ahead of the Angels' third baseman) were left off the first team. Perhaps most amazingly, Frank Oceak—who had led the Angels to the record-setting double-pennant season—was not chosen as manager of the year, that honor going to Denny Burns of third place Neosho.

Still, despite the *Times'* feeling that the Missourians had "ganged up" on Fayetteville, the Angels placed Oceak, Ed Checkley, George Bender, and Ripper Collins on the first team. Grosse, Hatch, Szuch, Rudy Briner, the departed Cliff Stebe, and Ray Parrott all made Honorable Mention.

In fairness, as Walter Lemke pointed out in his "Angel Food" column, perhaps the worst snub of all was that suffered by Neosho's Steve Greble. Greble had hit .320, led the league with 122 runs scored, and also topped the circuit with 22 home runs—yet he too had only made Honorable Mention.

With the regular season over and the All-Star team controversy behind them, Carthage and Fayetteville opened their playoff series on

Fayetteville Angels, 1939
Photo courtesy of University of Arkansas Digital Photo Collections Photo 3018

schedule, Wednesday, August 30. Five hundred fans came out to the Fair Grounds to watch their local favorites battle the Missourians in game one, but Carthage sent them home disappointed, beating Angels ace George Bender to take a 1-0 lead in the series.

The following day the Angels turned the table on the Pirates while the paper openly wondered, as they said fans did as well, why Fayetteville "who won everything possible during the regular season" had to be in any kind of playoff at all. Regardless of how little motivation they may have had, the Angels won the second game to even the series at one game apiece.

If fans and players were having trouble finding significance in the playoff series, imagine how they must have felt when on the very day that the second playoff game score was reported in the paper, September 1, 1939, the massive front-page banner headline of the *Times* declared: *"WAR REPORTED,"* and a subhead read *"NAZI ARMY RUSHED INTO POLAND."*

World War II had begun in earnest. The greatest conflagration the planet has ever seen had passed from the realm of hoped against possibility into devastating, destructive reality. The globe and the combatant nations upon it would never be the same.

The United States had not yet entered the fray, however, and the little playoff series in the little out-of-the-way Arkansas-Missouri League went on. Fayetteville lost on that memorable Friday, before 1,000 fans at Carthage, to go down two games to one to the Pirates.

Saturday and Sunday's games were also in Carthage (the first drew 1,250 fans, the second 2,000) but because the *Times* didn't put out a Sunday edition in those days, Fayetteville fans had to wait until Monday to read the results. They weren't good. Carthage had won both games by identical scores, 5-4, in virtually identical ways.

Saturday they beat the Angels when Carthage right fielder Harvey Beaster hit a solo home run with two out in the bottom of the ninth inning. They won again on Sunday when Pirates catcher John Pavlich drove in the winning run on a fielder's choice ground ball with one out in the bottom of the ninth inning. Carthage had taken the series four games to one and their fans cheered "long and hard" after each of the last two wins.

Despite the disappointing playoff outcome, Fayetteville supporters could take solace in the fact that the Angels had fought to the last; and although they came up a run short in each of those final two games, the series loss could not diminish the club's overall accomplishments.

This was the best team the town had ever had and they made 1939 the most exciting and memorable season in the history of professional baseball in Fayetteville.

EIGHT
1940: A Last, Short Season

FROM THE FALL of 1939 to the spring of 1940, news about the growing war in Europe was paramount in the broadcast and print media. Concerns about everyday life, such as whether or not the Arkansas-Missouri League or the Fayetteville franchise within it would continue, were naturally relegated to a secondary position. With England under siege and Hitler marching across the European continent, American eyes were focused on front pages where daily stories kept the nation abreast of the latest developments from around the world.

Yet despite the distressing global outlook, baseball in the little Arkansas-Missouri League carried on. As always, Fayetteville had to worry about finances, sponsorship, managers and players. In short—keep the franchise afloat. Early returns did not look favorable.

Just days after University of Arkansas president J. C. Futrall was killed in a tragic automobile accident and on the same day that J. W. Fulbright was named to replace him (Monday, September 18, 1939), a *Northwest Arkansas Times* sports page headline read: **"Fayetteville Probably Out of Ark-Mo Loop."**

League president Robert Henry, however, was not prepared to let the Fayetteville club go gently into that dark good night of baseball oblivion. On November 9, 1939, Henry indicated that both "Rogers and Siloam Springs might re-enter the league" if Fayetteville could "continue to hold a franchise."

Two days later, Fayetteville team officials called for local fan support and the *Times* declared: **"'Keep Baseball' Movement up to City's**

Fans." On November 23, President Henry said Siloam Springs would have a team in 1940 and that it "would be unthinkable for Fayetteville not to have a baseball team next year."

Less than a week later, on November 29, the *Times* reported: *"Baseball Club Plans to Keep Sport in City."* Fayetteville elected a completely new set of officers for the franchise, which now appeared to be a lock for a seventh season in the league. Bill Cain, V. James Ptak and others who had guided the club to three straight first-division finishes stepped aside. The new leaders were: Jim Bohart, president; R.U. Marshall, vice-president; and Bill McClain, secretary-treasurer.

By December 11, league president, Henry, had returned from the annual NAPBL mid-winter meeting held in Cincinnati with optimistic news. All three Missouri clubs in the Arkansas-Missouri League already had major league backing (Monett with the St. Louis Cardinals, Neosho with the New York Yankees, and Carthage with the Pittsburgh Pirates) and, Henry believed, the St. Louis Browns, Detroit Tigers and Brooklyn Dodgers were also leaning toward sponsoring clubs in the struggling circuit.

With its officers already chosen and the hope of sponsorship perhaps right around the corner, the Angels baseball club might have agreed with the December 30, 1939, front-page headline of the *Northwest Arkansas Times* that proclaimed: *"Fayetteville's Outlook Bright For 1940."*

Early in the new decade, baseball commissioner Landis made another ruling that made free agents of 91 players in the Detroit Tigers organization (including 87 minor leaguers). Happily, this decision did not affect the Arkansas-Missouri League or any of its franchises as the judge's earlier rulings had, but the survival of the Arkansas-Missouri League was still anything but certain. On March 7, 1940 a *Times* sports headline read: *"Life of Ark-Mo Depends Upon Fayetteville."*

According to the accompanying article, the St. Louis Cardinals would be willing to move their Monett club to Siloam Springs to balance out the teams in each state and to give Fayetteville a natural, local rival. Fayetteville had made it clear that they did not want to operate a franchise without another northwest Arkansas team in the league and, at a March 6 league meeting in Rogers, club representatives voted 3-1 in support of Fayetteville's position.[35] The Cardinals seemed to take the vote to heart, and by the end of the month, the Monett move to Siloam Springs was formalized.

At a March 24 meeting, Robert Henry was re-elected Arkansas-Missouri League president (Henry also would "direct" the posts of vice-president and secretary-treasurer) and it was reported that Fayetteville had been "assured" of financial aid by Judge Bramham of the NAPBL. For 1940, the league intended to use its standard 120-game schedule and to begin competitive play on May 2, after a short spring training starting April 20.

In the days leading up to the opening of spring training, Fayetteville learned that—as a *Times* headline for April 12 declared— *"Brooklyn Likely to Place Baseball Club in City."* This exciting news, coming on the heels of phone conversations between Angels officials and Dodgers General Manager Larry MacPhail, was printed the same day that Brooklyn scout, Howard "Ducky" Holmes, blew into Fayetteville to size the locals up for sponsorship by the big league club. Holmes' one-day whirlwind visit was not only loud and blustery but would leave a season long trail of debris in its wake.

Ducky, who was quoted as being "Well satisfied" with the Angels, had several conditions for Brooklyn sponsorship. Instead of relying on fan and merchant donations, for example, Ducky insisted that Fayetteville sell about 250 thirty-game tickets (at $10.20 per booklet, a $1.53 savings for fans over game day tickets) to establish a financial base for the season.

Holmes also wanted the ballpark to be in good shape (work had been done to improve the Fair Grounds field back in late March) and have a good set of lights, and he wanted the club to provide a separate restroom for lady fans.

If Fayetteville would do all this and come up with $1500 for him ($800 more than any league club could afford, it was estimated), Ducky would additionally deign to manage the club himself for the

1940 season. Despite the unexpected demands, Fayetteville needed the Brooklyn sponsorship and so the locals met the Dodgers' requirements—except for hiring Ducky as manager.

On Thursday, April 18, the front page of the *Times* displayed a photograph of Judge V. James Ptak giving Mayor A.D. McAllister a receipt beneath a headline reading: *"Mayor Buys First Baseball Ticket Book."* Having gained the mayor's endorsement and buoyed by an unofficial *Times* survey indicating fan support for the thirty-game booklet promotion, Fayetteville committed itself to meet the Dodgers' primary sponsorship demand.

With sponsorship finally settled and the regular season opener just around the corner, it was time to get down to the business of baseball. The Chamber of Commerce announced it would help defray the cost of spring training for the Angels and the Junior Chamber of Commerce signed on as sponsors for the May 2 regular season home opener against Siloam Springs.

On April 25, about a dozen Brooklyn minor leaguers arrived in Fayetteville from a Dodgers farm club training camp in Murfreesboro, Tennessee. Their arrival signaled the start of a rapid and very abbreviated spring training.

Just three days after the new Angels players arrived in town, they played the Fayetteville Junior Legion team in a rain-shortened practice game highlighted by a home run by Junior's catcher and former Angels' batboy, Sherman Lollar. Meanwhile, returning veteran Pete Ashmore was leading the Angels while the club waited for the arrival of their new player-manager Charles "Herb" Fash. Fash had starred in the Class B Southeastern League in 1939 (a first baseman, he batted .337 for Mobile, Alabama while fielding at an outstanding .998 clip).

"Angels Open Baseball Menu Tonight" read the large front-page headline in the *Times* for Thursday, May 2, 1940. The game, against long-time rival and re-entrant into the league, Siloam Springs, was scheduled to begin at 8 p.m. with the Fayetteville High School band performing before the first pitch, which was to be tossed out by Mayor McAllister.

The Angels, sponsored by the Dodgers through their Dayton Wings team of the Class C Middle Atlantic League started the following lineup:

John "Angel" Bauer	3B
Mike Daugherty	CF
Pete Ashmore	SS
Raymond Luke	1B
John Coppinger	LF
Al Giovanetti	2B
Bill "Whitey" Johnson	C
John Henry Homesley	RF
Ralph Prater	P

Perhaps opening night was a harbinger of how the 1940 season would turn out. Fayetteville won the game, shutting out Siloam Springs 3-0 before 900 cold fans at the Fair Grounds. Traditionally, Fayetteville usually lost their first and last games of the year (including split seasons, when they had twice the opportunities) and for the last three seasons they had fielded very competitive teams in a hard playing, competitive league. But this year, atypically, they won that first game. In Neosho, the Yankees defeated the Carthage Pirates to complete opening night in the Ark–Mo League.

Including the opening night victory, the Angels played .500 ball (4-4) for the first eight games of the season. The results were average, but the scores themselves were often extraordinary. Over a five-day stretch Fayetteville was involved in four high scoring contests. The first of these was an 18-2 loss at Siloam Springs, May 3, in which Angels' pitchers gave up thirteen bases on balls. After a "normal" 5-3 loss at Carthage the next day, the Angels beat the Pirates 18-10 back home at the Fair Grounds on May 5 despite committing eight errors.

Neosho then pounded Fayetteville 15-2 at the Fair Grounds and 19-1 at Neosho May 7. In the latter game, Fayetteville made an unbelievable thirteen errors and the *Times* reported that Manager Fash—

who had finally shown up to take control of the squad from acting pilot Ashmore—was looking at some new players.[36]

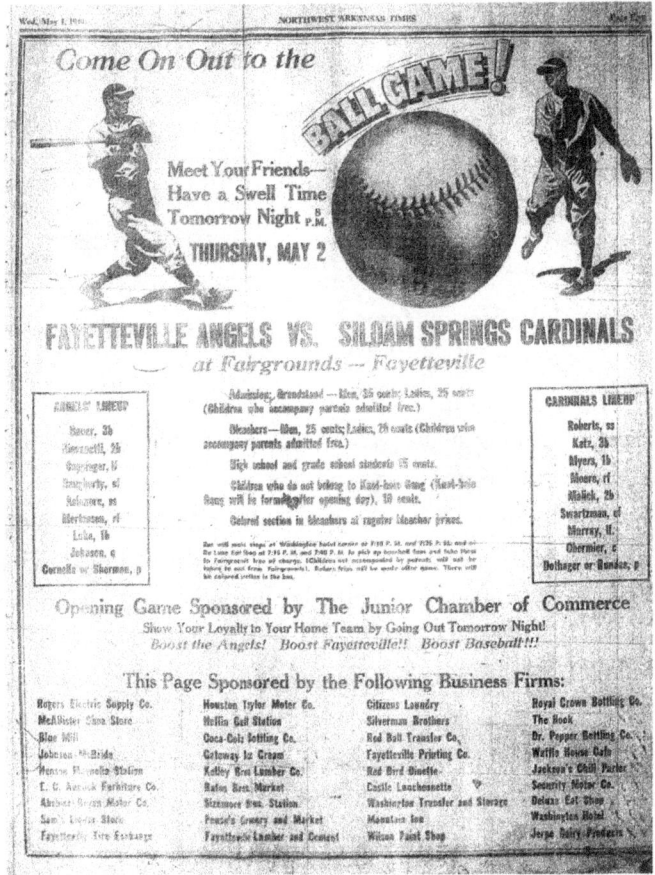

Season Opening Ad, 1940: *Fayetteville Daily Democrat*

On May 8, before a tiny crowd at the Fair Grounds, Fash made his first appearance as a player in an Angels win over Neosho. The next day, Fayetteville beat Siloam Springs 3-0 on the road behind the one-hit pitching of "Farmer" Joe Prylich. The Angels committed only one error, but another play—which was disputed and may have been another error—was ruled a hit and cost Prylich a no-hit masterpiece.

Fairgrounds Ballpark in Fayetteville, 1951
Photo courtesy of University of Arkansas Razorback Annual

After the win at Siloam Springs, Fayetteville lost four in a row and by mid-month were dead last in the league. The only bright spots for the team were the pitching of Prylich and the acquisition of new uniforms from the team's direct minor league sponsor, the Dayton Wings. Unfortunately, the team couldn't wear the new "unis" (which bore the name "Wings" on them) right away because they lacked matching socks and caps.

For the last two weeks of May, Fayetteville played mediocre ball going 7-8. Besides struggling with opposing teams, the Angels had to battle the elements (suffering three rainouts in five days and a steady diet of cold evenings) and found themselves playing before a seriously dwindling fan base. Only 88 paying customers showed up for the Siloam Springs game at the Fair Grounds on Saturday, May 25.

On May 29, ace pitcher Joe Prylich got his sixth win of the season without a loss, beating Neosho at the Fair Grounds 8-1, and the following day the Angels claimed another victory at Siloam Springs. The Cardinals did, however, end the month and a six-game losing streak with it by defeating Fayetteville at the Fair Grounds on May 31.

June opened with Carthage leading the league by just one and a half games over Siloam Springs, despite the Cardinals recent losing streak. Neosho held third place while Fayetteville was last. To match their lowly standing, the Angels lost the first two games of June (three losses in a row overall) first at Neosho on June 1 and then June 2 at home against Carthage.

The latter game saw Joe Prylich lose his first game of the year (to fall to 6-1) and the *Times* declared in a headline *"New Suits Jinx to Prylich and Angels."* This was the first game in which the Angels wore their new uniforms and waggish sportswriter, Carl Bell, wrote (referring to the name Wings emblazoned on the team's uniforms) that "the Angels have finally sprouted wings."[37]

The Tuesday, June 4, *Northwest Arkansas Times* carried some good news, Fayetteville had soundly beaten Siloam Springs 16-2 on Monday night at Siloam Springs, and some bad news. The club, it was reported, had had its "most disastrous May in the seven-year-old" history of the franchise, losing money on "all the games played from May 15 through June 1."

Despite inclement weather and poor crowds, the Angels managed to keep winning about half the time, and on Friday night, June 7 they again trounced Siloam Springs at the Fair Grounds 28-6. The team had 21 hits and set an all-time league scoring record with their 28 runs. Pete Ashmore set a probable league record by driving in ten runs, seven of those coming on two home runs.

Unfortunately, the good baseball news was overshadowed by more bad financial information. It was formally announced at the game that the franchise had lost money on nearly every game during May and that the club might be lost as well. They needed $500 to keep the team afloat and donations were requested from fans.

Team officials also, for the first time, blamed Ducky Holmes and his ticket book sales scheme for part of their financial problems. Additionally, they pointed out that Ducky's bosses in Brooklyn had said they would purchase the club outright but reneged on the deal and made it just a working agreement.

To counteract poor attendance, the team began putting on a series of 10¢ Ladies Nights and other such promotions and provided free bus service to and from games. The shuttle ran from the Washington Hotel on the square to the DeLuxe Eat Shop on Dickson Street[38] then out to the ballpark and back by the same route after the game. Continued rainouts and minimal fan support, however, continued to take a toll on the struggling franchise.

Only a "handful of fans" were at the Fair Grounds on Sunday, June 9, to watch Fayetteville and Neosho split one of the more interesting double-headers in the history of the Arkansas-Missouri League. Both contests were seven inning affairs and were played very quickly (the first in one hour even, the second fifteen minutes longer).

In the first game, Walter Nasalik of Neosho became the first and only Arkansas-Missouri League pitcher to ever pitch a no-hitter and lose. The Angels scored one run on a walk and three errors to best Nasalik 1-0. In the second game, Fayetteville was defeated 6-0, getting a lone single from left fielder Joe "Red" Cornella to give the home team just one base hit in the entire doubleheader.

From June 10 to June 17, Angels' games were rained out five times. The team was getting bogged down—both figuratively and literally. Towards the end of the wet spell, on June 15, the paper reported that Bill McClain had become the new president of the Angels, replacing acting-president Jim Bohart who had been promoted to editor of the *Times* and would not be able to do both jobs.

When the rains did finally let up, the Angels resumed their average play, losing the first game of a Fair Grounds doubleheader to Carthage on June 18 and then dropping a decision at Siloam Springs the next day. "Farmer" Joe Prylich, however, was anything but average—as usual. He shut out Carthage in the second June 18 game, then bested Siloam Springs on the road June 23 to run his record to 9-1. In the Carthage win, manager Fash, leader of the "Fashmen" as the papers liked to say, hit an inside the park home run which was lost—in typical Arkansas-Missouri League fashion—in the tall outfield grass.

On Tuesday, June 25, club fortunes took yet another turn for the worse. New Fayetteville president McClain announced that, for the club to continue fielding a team, it needed $600 by Friday to pay back salaries and transportation costs. McClain cited bad weather and poor ticket sales for the franchise's financial problems.

Two days later the *Times* ran a front-page story with the headline *"City Probably Will Lose Club."* Local "civic minded" men's clubs held a meeting but failed to reach agreement on a bail out plan for the Angels. Club president Bill McClain reportedly contacted league president Henry and Brooklyn Dodgers General Manager Larry MacPhail with regard to Fayetteville's dire economic situation.

The next day, June 28, 1940, a *Times* sports page headline gave local fans the bad news: *"Fayetteville Franchise Turned Over to League."* The article explained that negotiations were under way to have either original league member, Rogers or Nevada, Missouri, take over the club and the following day it appeared that Rogers would get the team.

Although a group of Rogers businessmen, headed by J. O. Clark, tried to gain leadership of the Fayetteville franchise, they were unable to get the backing needed to do so, and the team was never actually transferred from Fayetteville.

The financial difficulties of the franchise clearly affected the baseball team. From June 24 through June 27 they lost four in a row, including three times to Neosho. The second of those three losses was an eleven-inning defeat on June 25 in what would be the last Arkansas-Missouri League game ever played at the Fair Grounds.

A home game against Siloam Springs scheduled for Friday, June 28, was rained out and a game the following night against Carthage was canceled. As it turned out, there would be no more professional games in Fayetteville that year—or any other.

In spite of all the problems in Fayetteville, the league chose an All-Star team and scheduled a contest pitting Arkansas players against their Missouri counterparts for Monday, July 1, in Carthage. The Angels, though nestled in last place, placed catcher Bill "Whitey" Johnson, pitchers Ralph Prater and Joe Prylich, infielders Joe Cornella, Glenn Calloway and Herb Fash, and utility man Caesar "Skee" Russo on the Arkansas squad.

On Saturday, June 29, Fayetteville traveled to Siloam Springs and beat the Cardinals 7-0 for the last win in team history.[39] On Sunday, June 30, Carthage won 12-2 at Siloam Springs and Fayetteville lost at Neosho 10-8.

The latter was Fayetteville's last professional baseball game and, along with the Carthage-Siloam Springs game, constituted the last games ever played in the Arkansas State/Arkansas-Missouri League.

A large *Northwest Arkansas Times* sports page banner headline for July 1, 1940 read: "Ark-Mo League Folds Up for 1940 Season."

Fayetteville had staggered, as could be expected, to a 1-5 mark in their last six games, but still somehow managed to end up third in the league, one-half game ahead of Siloam Springs. Carthage easily outdistanced Neosho to win the abbreviated 1940 pennant by ten and one-half games.

The final standings were:

Arkansas-Missouri League
(Final Standings—League Folded)

Team	Won	Lost	Pct
Carthage	37	18	.673
Neosho	27	29	.482
Fayetteville	21	29	.420
Siloam Springs	21	30	.412

Even with all the problems in Fayetteville and the final collapse of the league, the All-Star game went on as scheduled the night of July 1 in Carthage. The Arkansas squad took the measure of the Missourians, 9-4, before a "large" crowd. That final contest, as described in the *Times*, "officially closed the Arkansas-Missouri League season for 1940."

Despite league president Henry's hope to "form a stronger circuit in 1941," the abrupt, shortened conclusion to the 1940 season did in fact bring the curtain down forever on the Arkansas State/Arkansas-Missouri League. In doing so, it also put an end to professional baseball in Fayetteville for the rest of the century and possibly for all time.

Carthage Pirates, 1940
Photo courtesy of John G. Hall

EPILOGUE

IN THE SUMMER of 1940, after a rocky six and one-half year run, professional baseball died out in Fayetteville, and it has never come back. Looking back from the vantage point of so many years in the future, there's a poignancy about the old Arkansas-Missouri League and the Fayetteville Angels having faded into a virtual black hole of obscurity.

The raucous, rowdy sounds of wood on horsehide, of called strikes and balls and outs, of joyous shouts of victory and unhappy cries of defeat, these are now no more than a faint almost lost echo barely floating somewhere in the ether of forgotten history.

Yet in the immediate aftermath of the collapse of the Arkansas-Missouri League, as players and managers fanned out through the country to find other positions in baseball,[40] this tiny Class D league in the backwoods of the Ozark Mountains was important enough for the premier baseball magazine of the time, *The Sporting News,* to send one of its reporters out to see why the league failed.

Frederick G. Lieb came to the area and interviewed fans and officials in all the towns of the league. What Lieb reported was what had already pretty much been determined: the Arkansas-Missouri League folded in 1940 because Fayetteville folded and Fayetteville folded because of poor attendance, due in large part to bad weather, and because of bad advice the club got and took from Brooklyn Dodgers scout Ducky Holmes. The refusal of Dodgers General Manager Larry MacPhail to provide economic support to Fayetteville when they desperately needed it was the final nail in the Angels' coffin.[41]

The Arkansas-Missouri was the first minor league in six years to start a season and not finish it. Historically, this put the loop at the vanguard of the continuing economic crises and developing international conflicts that would virtually wipe out minor league baseball in the United States during the upcoming years of World War II.

As such, this tiny league was emblematic both of the rise and fall of the minor leagues in this epoch and also of the difficulty of sustaining an enterprise through the depression and keeping it afloat when the country's resources were being redirected toward an impending global war.

What then is the point of presenting the story of an obscure minor league baseball team in a small town in a poor, out of the way section of the Arkansas Ozarks? Why go to the trouble to remember it at all?

Besides the intrinsic value of any record of human endeavor, no matter how insignificant or seemingly irrelevant it might appear, the story of Fayetteville's baseball team, and of the small league to which it belonged, is a reflection of the larger time in which it existed.

The annals of Fayetteville's Angels (and its Educators and Bears before them) reveal something of the history of the city, the region, the nation, and the era itself. In following the all-but-forgotten days and games of these men and teams, we see again, in a dynamic, fresh and vibrant way, the very essence of one of the most extraordinary periods in American history.

In the comical concern of league officials for the cost, care, and complete and full use of every single precious baseball put in or out of play, we see the very serious and necessary significance placed on any physical resource during this period of extreme economic hardship. We also see in the organizations, fans, and officials of the league the qualities that helped the U.S. find its way out of the Great Depression and to victory in World War II.

Despite the many difficulties that the era presented on and off the field, the Arkansas-Missouri League reflected an unwavering optimism, a toughness in the face of adversity, a can-do attitude towards solving problems, and a sense of humor and perspective about the world, the country, and the little Class D baseball league for which they gave their best. In the end, however, the Fayetteville Angels and the Arkansas-Missouri League could not survive.

Yet, even these many decades later, the old Angels and their rugged little minor league can still be entertaining to us, and not only to fans of baseball in general but also to those interested in reading and learning about local history as well.

"Where else," Walter Lemke wrote in 1952, "in the…history of organized baseball can you find a one-armed umpire and a one-eyed umpire, a barefoot pitcher" and "a woman playing an entire game of league ball?"[42]

The answer, of course—as Lemke himself knew—was nowhere. The experience of the little Arkansas-Missouri League and of the Fayetteville team within it, common as that experience was in a larger, broader sense, was in the particular sense unique to its time and place. And as long as the story of that time, place and people remains alive, its spirit remains alive as well.

The sounds of both fan and player, of wooden bats hitting leather-covered baseballs, these still echo—however faintly—down through time to us. After all these years, after all these lost decades, there still are—in the joy of young people playing baseball and in the character of the region—Angels in the Ozarks.

APPENDICES

APPENDIX A
Arkansas State/Arkansas-Missouri League
Overview

Arkansas State League (1934-1935) / Arkansas-Missouri League (1936-1940) Teams

1934	1935	1936	1937	1938	1939	1940
Fayetteville Educators	Fayetteville Bears	Fayetteville Bears	Fayetteville Angels	Fayetteville Angels	Fayetteville Angels	Fayetteville Angels
Siloam Springs Buffaloes	Siloam Springs Travelers	Siloam Springs Travelers	Siloam Springs Travelers	Siloam Springs Travelers		Siloam Springs Cardinals
Rogers Rustlers	Rogers Cardinals	Rogers Lions	Rogers Lions	Rogers Reds		
Bentonville Officeholders	Bentonville Officeholders	Bentonville Mustangs				
	Huntsville Red Birds					
	Cassville Tigers	Cassville Blues				
		Monett Red Birds	Monett Red Birds	Monett Red Birds	Monett Red Birds	
			Neosho Night Hawks	Neosho Yankees	Neosho Yankees	Neosho Yankees
			*Vinita, Oklahoma	Carthage Pirates	Carthage Pirates	Carthage Pirates

Vinita dropped out of the league the day before the 1937 season began

Arkansas State League (1934-1935)/ Arkansas-Missouri League (1936-1940)

Teams, Managers, Major League (ML) Affiliation

1934	Arkansas State League	4 Teams
Team	**Managers**	**Major League Affiliation***
Fayetteville Educators	Fred Hawn/Frank Mathews	
Bentonville Officeholders	"Red" Wilson/Tom McGill/Ed Hawk(s)	
Siloam Springs Buffaloes	Clyde Glass	
Rogers Rustlers	Ed Hawk(s)/Pete Casey	

*League operated independently, but under watchful eye of St. Louis Cardinals

1935	Arkansas State League	6 Teams
Team	**Managers**	**Major League Affiliation****
Fayetteville Bears	Pete Casey/Fred Cato	
Bentonville Officeholders	Wilbur Davis	
Siloam Springs Travelers	Ray Powell	
Rogers Cardinals	Fred Cato/J. O. Clark	
Huntsville Red Birds	Jim Nicely/Charley Wilson/Bill Werner	
Cassville, Mo, Tigers	Ed Hawk(s)	

**League operated by St. Louis Cardinals through their Springfield, MO farm club.

1936	Arkansas-Missouri League	6 Teams
Team	**Managers**	**Major League Affiliation**
Fayetteville Bears	Fred Hawn	St. Louis Cardinals
Bentonville Mustangs	Art Hauger	Independent
Siloam Springs Travelers	Ray Powell	Cincinnati Reds
Rogers Lions	Homer "Doc" Ledbetter/ Frank Stapleton	New York Yankees
Monett, Mo, Red Birds	Adolf "Buzz" Arlitt/ Ken Blackman	St. Louis Cardinals
Cassville, Mo, Blues	Gary Coker/Clifford Day/ Erwin "Zeke" Gansauer	New York Yankees

1937   Arkansas-Missouri League   5 Teams

Team	Managers	Major League Affiliation
Fayetteville Angels	Fred Hawn/Ken Blackman	St. Louis Cardinals
Siloam Springs Travelers	Ray Powell	St. Louis Browns
Rogers Lions	Ted Mayer	New York Yankees
Monett, Mo, Red Birds	Ken Blackman/Joe Davis	St. Louis Cardinals
Neosho, Mo, Night Hawks	Denny Burns	Independent
Vinita, OK	*(dropped out day before season opened)*	

1938   Arkansas-Missouri League   6 Teams

Team	Managers	Major League Affiliation
Fayetteville Angels	Cliff "Bud" Knox	Independent
Siloam Springs Travelers	Vincent "Moon" Mullen/ Runt Marr/Mike Sertich	St. Louis Browns
Rogers Reds	Lester "Pat" Patterson	Cincinnati Reds
Monett, Mo, Red Birds	Heinie Mueller	St. Louis Cardinals
Neosho, Mo, Yankees	Denny Burns	New York Yankees
Carthage, Mo, Pirates	Adolph "Buzz" Arlitt	Pittsburgh Pirates

1939   Arkansas-Missouri League   4 Teams

Team	Managers	Major League Affiliation
Fayetteville Angels	Frank Oceak	St. Louis Browns
Monett, Mo, Red Birds	Fred Hawn	St. Louis Cardinals
Neosho, Mo, Yankees	Denny Burns	New York Yankees
Carthage, Mo, Pirates	Adolph "Buzz" Arlitt	Pittsburgh Pirates

1940   Arkansas-Missouri League   4 Teams

Team	Managers	Major League Affiliation
Fayetteville Angels	Charles "Herb" Fash	Brooklyn Dodgers
Siloam Springs Cardinals	Herb Moore	St. Louis Cardinals
Neosho, MO, Yankees	Ed Grayston	New York Yankees
Cathage, MO, Pirates	Adolph "Buzz" Arlitt	Pittsburgh Pirates

[League suspended play 7/1/40]

APPENDIX B
Arkansas State/Arkansas-Missouri League
Yearly Champions

Split Season

Year	First Half	Second Half	Playoff
1934	Rogers[1]	Bentonville	*Rogers, 4/3 over Bentonville*
1935	Rogers	Siloam Springs	*Rogers, 4/3 over Siloam Springs*
1936	Cassville	Siloam Springs	*Siloam Springs, 4/3 over Cassville[2]*

Full Season

Year			
1937	Rogers		*Rogers, 4/1 over Fayetteville*
1938	Neosho		*Carthage, 4/1 over Neosho*

Split Season

Year	First Half	Second Half	Playoff
1939	Fayetteville	Fayetteville[3]	*Carthage, 4/1 over Fayetteville*
1940	Carthage	*Leading when League disbanded July 1*	

Notes:
[1] *Rogers won one game playoff over Siloam Springs to win first half of 1934 season*
[2] *Plus one tie*
[3] *Fayetteville was the only club to ever win both halves of a split season*

APPENDIX C
Arkansas State/Arkansas-Missouri League
Yearly League Leaders

1934 Arkansas State League Leaders[43]

HITTERS

BA		H		R		2B	
Graves	.387	Rushing	96	Beams	61	Glass	19
Glass	.374	Beams	87	Allum	59	Stapleton	19
Beams	.340	Homan	87	Graves	59	Rushing	17
Woodrow	.333	Glass	86	Rushing	51	Allum	13
Rushing	.321	Graves	86	Foster	48	Beams	13
Homan	.319	Nicely	77	Johnson	48	Homan	13
Ensley	.300	Thomas	76	Woodrow	48	Watson	13

3B		HR		RBI		SB	
Glass	12	Beams	12	Glass	67	Homan	25
Graves	10	Rushing	9	Rushing	55	Nicely	22
Homan	9	Homan	8	Beams	52	Ensley	19
Beams	8	Lindquist	8	Graves	52	Foster	18
Rushing	8	Nicely	8	Fair	46	Yourchak	15
Lindquist	7	Woodrow	8	Stapleton	45	Scott	12
Watson	6	Ensley	7	Landthrip	42	Bush	11
Woodrow	6	Fair	7	Lindquist	40	Glass	7
		Graves	7				

PITCHERS

WINS		PCT	
Wollard	12-3	Hill	8-1 (.889)
Lakin	11-10	Wollard	12-3 (.800)
Young	10-5	Young	10-5 (.667)
J. White	10-7	J. White	10-7 (.589)
Rorie	10-10	Lakin	11-10 (.524)
Buchanan	10-14	Rorie	10-10 (.500)

1935 Arkansas State League Leaders[44]

HITTERS

BA		H		R		2B	
Kratzer	.397	W. Davis	146	Roberts	89	Turner	31
M. Johnson	.386	Roberts	140	Turner	87	Stapleton	27
Roberts	.364	Stapleton	139	Parks	84	Cooper	26
Cooper	.359	Turner	130	Stapleton	84	Fredericks	23
W. Davis	.354	Ludwig	124	Mabry	81	M. Johnson	23
Woodrow	.345	M. Johnson	122	Fair	80	D. White	23
Casey	.344	Cooper	120	Thomas	79	Bosse	22
Stapleton	.340	Thomas	120	D. White	76	Villipique	22
Thomas	.340	D. White	120			Woodrow	22
Ledbetter	.340						

3B		HR		RBI		SB	
Turner	14	Roberts	21	W. Davis	93	Turner	43
M. Johnson	13	Fair	20	Roberts	89	Parks	37
Roberts	12	Woodrow	15	Cooper	79	Fair	30
Stapleton	12	Cooper	14	Woodrow	77	Woodrow	28
Fair	10	Mabry	13	Turner	76	Kratzer	26
Werner	10	W. Davis	12	Fair	75	Wyer	25
		Harvatin	12	J. Davis	74	Villipique	23
		Werner	12			Watkins	23

PITCHERS

WINS		PCT.		ERA	
W. Brown	13-5	J. Murray	11-2 (.864)	Gayer	2.68
Fralick	13-6	W. Brown	13-5 (.722)	W. Brown	2.97
Hill	13-7	John	11-5 (.688)	Hill	3.07
Tisdale	13-7	Reszenski	11-5 (.688)	C. Wilson	3.10
Langston	13-11	C. Wilson	11-5 (.688)	J. Murray	3.28
Gibson	12-12	Fralick	13-6 (.684)	Fralick	3.37
Raper	12-12	Hill	13-7 (.650)	Tisdale	3.77
		Tisdale	13-7 (.650)	Gansauer	3.84

CG		IP		SO		BB	
Hill	18	Gansauer	229	John	147	Hill	74
Fralick	17	Langston	196	W. Brown	145	Jensen	74
Raper	16	Gibson	191	Gibson	145	Tisdale	75
Gansauer	15	Tisdale	191	Langston	138	W. Brown	87
Gayer	15	Hill	179	Tisdale	126	A. White	87
W. Brown	14	Raper	174	Fralick	124	John	109
Swank	12	Fralick	172	Gansauer	123	Gibson	112

1936 Arkansas State League Leaders[45]

HITTERS

BA		H		R		2B	
Rock	.3333*	Lewis	164	Lewis	130	Neighbors	29
Lewis	.3326	Tucker	158	Tone	106	Arlitt	27
Klier	.329	Lutz	155	Fair	104	Lutz	27
D. White	.328	Tone	152	Tucker	102	Klier	25
Lutz	.322	Klier	148	Villipique	93	Tone	25
Ledbetter	.320	Villipique	147	Crawford	90	Tucker	25
Tucker	.318	D. White	145	Ludwig	90	Watkins	24
Arlitt	.316					Werner	24
Tone	.316						

*Closest batting race ever, also the lowest leading hitting average ever

3B		HR		RBI		SB	
Klier	14	Lewis	28*	Tone	125	Tone	45
Lewis	13	Fair	21	Lewis	95	Tucker	43
Robinson	11	Honea	20	Arlitt	93	Fair	39
Lutz	10	Arlitt	18	McCarty	86	Crawford	35
McCarty	10	Neighbors	16	Neighbors	86	Ledbetter	27
Tone	10	Tone	16	Fair	84	Lewis	27
Villipique	10	Ashmore	15	Ludwig	81	Raper	27
		Werner	15	D. White	81		

* Most ever home runs in one season

PITCHERS

WINS		PCT		ERA	
Raper	23-7*	Murray	15-4 (.788)	Murray	1.35*
Strunk	19-7	Raper	23-7 (.766)	Raper	2.06
Gansauer	17-10	Strunk	19-7 (.730)	Terry	2.84
Murray	15-4	Terry	14-8 (.636)	R. Clark	2.88
Langston	15-10	Gansauer	17-10 (.630)	H. Davis	2.94
Terry	14-8	Langston	15-10 (.600)	Smalling	3.00
H. Davis	13-10	Smalling	12-8 (.600)	Langston	3.06

* Both figures indicated are All-Time League bests

IP		SO		BB	
Gansauer	255	Olson	163	Potts	117
Raper	249	Hawkins	145	C. Neighbors	108
Olson	231	Gansauer	138	Gore	106
R. Clark	231	Potts	136	Cross	91
Gerhauser	227	R. Clark	132	Gerhauser	90
Langston	226	Strunk	119	Hawkins	86
H. Davis	223	Langston	118	Roth	82

1937 Arkansas State League Leaders[46]

HITTERS

BA		H		R		2B	
Evans	.385	Fugit	183	Priddy	109	Lutz	38
Fugit	.374	Lutz	158	McCarron	96	Fugit	35
Mayer	.340	Sams	154	Sams	92	Westover	30
Priddy	.336	Priddy	153	Milani	89	Ashmore	27
Lutz	.335	Troupe	143	Watkins	86	Wolverton	27
Blackman	.330	Wolverton	143	Lutz	83	Troupe	26
Milani	.323	Milani	141	Fugit	80	Priddy	25
						Sams	25

3B		HR		RBI		SB	
Evans	13	Gibson	20	Sams	99	Priddy	23
Troupe	13	Hundley	12	Gibson	92	Gold	22
Kreuger	11	Myers	11	Fugit	85	Hundley	22
Priddy	10	Autry	10	Hundley	84	Sams	21
Boyce	9	Harvatin	10	Priddy	83	Watkins	20
Wolverton	9	Priddy	10	Lutz	81	Boyce	18
Blackman	8	Sams	10	Kreuger	78	Blackman	18
McCarron	8					Lutz	18

PITCHERS

WINS		PCT		ERA	
Hanning	16-7	Nelson	11-3 (.786)	Hanning	1.63
Derry	16-8	Hanning	16-7 (.696)	Nelson	2.18
Cross	14-8	Derry	16-8 (.667)	Smith	2.87
Collmeyer	13-7	Sinay	12-6 (.667)	Cross	2.93
Sinay	12-6	Ketcher	10-5 (.667)	Malesky	2.97
White	12-10	Collmeyer	13-7 (.667)	Collmeyer	3.25
Tarrant	12-14	Cross	14-8 (.636)	Sinay	3.42

CG		IP		SO		BB	
Tarrant	20	Cook	215	Smith	179	Hanning	28
Derry	19	Tarrant	196	Cook	155	Burns	38
Burns	18	Derry	192	Hanning	144	Collmeyer	42
Cook	18	Speer	187	Collmeyer	133	Cross	44
Hanning	18	Odneal	186	Odneal	126	Sinay	44
White	15	Burns	184	Derry	122	Livingston	55
		Burse	183	Tarrant	121	Smith	60

1938 Arkansas State League Leaders[47]

HITTERS

BA		H		R		2B	
Moran	.392	Wolverton	160	Luby	127	Moran	43
Seal	.367	Moran	159	VanSickel	124	Wolverton	35
E. Knoblauch	.356	Seal	158	Wolverton	120	Zielenski	34
Dusak	.351	Daluga	152	Lawrence	113	Lurtz	32
Kramer	.345	Swab	151	Arlitt	108	Scwab	32
James	.344	Arlitt	149	Moran	107	Arlitt	31
Arlitt	.342	Jansen	145	Silebar	101	Fowler	29
Jansen	.342					Silebar	29
						Sertich	29

3B		HR		RBI		SB	
Kreuger	16	Moran	22	Arlitt	132	Luby	76
Serpa	14	Naylor	19	Moran	114	Owen	55
Luby	13	Dusak	18	Naylor	94	Zielenski	41
Lurtz	13	Arlitt	17	Owen	92	I.Knoblauch	35
David	12	Knox	17	Kreuger	91	Daluga	34
Moran	12	Davis	14	Kommy	90	Kommy	34
Sertich	11	Kreuger	14	Serpa	90		
		Schwab	14				

PITCHERS

WINS		PCT		ERA	
Gill	20-3	Gill	20-3 (.870)	Gill	2.80
Toenes	19-10	Burns	11-3 (.787)	Burns	3.05
Deller	18-5	Deller	18-5 (.783)	Boham	3.09
Boham	16-5	Boham	16-5 (.765)	Deller	3.29
Heyne	16-10	Costello	14-5 (.737)	Costello	3.31
Costello	14-5	Drasites	14-5 (.737)	Heyne	3.42
Drasites	14-5	Wagenhurst	13-6 (.684)	Drasites	3.63
Skidgel	14-10			Skidgel	3.63

CG		IP		SO		BB	
Toenes	22	Toenes	249	Gill	266	Deller	49
Gill	21	Boham	218	Skidgel	230	Drasites	54
Deller	20	Heyne	210	Toenes	195	Blessing	58
Heyne	18	Skidgel	208	Williams	182	Wagenhurst	58
Boham	17	Deller	205	Costello	169	Heyne	61
Skidgel	17	Gill	199	Boham	167	Parker	66
Costello	15	Williams	199	Deller	161	Gill	70

1939 Arkansas State League Leaders[48]

HITTERS

BA		H		R		2B	
Arlitt	.358	Beaster	171	Greble	129	Sarver	40
Beaster	.353	Grosse	155	Grosse	115	Beaster	37
Hatch	.342	Szuch	155	Sarver	113	Szuch	31
Parrott	.335	Arlitt	148	Szuch	107	Hatch	30
Grosse	.333	Hatch	138	Beaster	101	Paul	29
Buerkholtz	.333	Greble	137	Hatch	100	Arlitt	28
Pavlich	.330	Harris	137	Owen	99	Greble	27
						Owen	27
						Pavlich	27

3B		HR		RBI		SB	
Buerkholtz	9	Greble	24	Arlitt	106	Sarver	48
Harris	8	Paul	16	Paul	97	Owen	44
Jansen	8	Arlitt	15	Greble	95	Greble	37
Sarver	8	Pavlich	14	Szuch	90	Grosse	30
Checkley	7	C.Knoblauch	11	Pavlich	83	Sackovich	29
C.Knoblauch	7	Barnhar	10	Owen	81	Bankhead	27
Szuch	7	Owen	10	Briner	76	Houk	27

PITCHERS

WINS		PCT		ERA	
Bender	20-4	Bender	20-4 (.833)	Bender	2.35
Horton	19-7	Deller	13-4 (.765)	Deller	2.56
Stebe	17-9	Horton	19-7 (.731)	Stebe	2.85
Lally	16-13	Odneal	13-6 (.684)	Playfair	3.50
Messerly	15-13	Stebe	17-9 (.654)	Lally	3.59
R.Smith	14-12	Narieka	11-6 (.647)	Horton	3.59
Deller	13-4	Barbolla	12-8 (.600)	Peterlich	3.68
Odneal	13-6				

CG		IP		SO		BB	
Bender	24	Lally	218	Bender	208	Deller	18
Lally	21	Peterlic	215	Lally	197	Green	31
Peterlic	21	Bender	210	Messerly	183	Playfair	44
Horton	19	R. Smit	208	R. Smit	172	Horton	48
R. Smith	18	Messerly	202	Odneal	160	Dothager	55
Deller	16	Horton	198	Stebe	140	Bender	60
Karas	16	Odneal	187	Peterlic	138	Narieka	64
Messerly	16	Wieneke	187	Barbolla	134	Sommerer	65
Stebe	16	Stebe	186	Horton	112	Wieneke	67

1940 Arkansas State League Leaders[49]

HITTERS*

BA		H		R		2B	
Fash**	.366	Gibson	72	Gibson	55	Dabbs	18
Arlitt	.360	Arlitt	71	Harris	54	Fash	18
Calloway	.333	Castiglione	70	Griffin	51	Amsberg	13
Gibson	.313	Harris	61	Arlitt	46	Arlitt	13
Griffin	.310	Amsberg	60	Swartzman	44	Castiglione	13
Barnett	.300	Grayston	59	Bankhead	41	Gibson	13
Amsberg	.299	Griffin	58	Grayston	41	Grayston	13
Castiglione	.299	Bankhead	56	Alford	39	Peterson	13
Peterson	.299	Myers	56	Peterson	38	Wiegand	12
Ashmore***	.296	Fash	56			Griffin	10

3B		HR		RBI		SB	
Gibson	8	Arlitt	12	Arlitt	58	Bankhead	22
Dabbs	6	Ashmore	9	Gibson	46	Arlitt	13
Daugherty	6	Alford	6	Amsberg	44	Grayston	11
Harris	5	Myers	6	Myers	43	Harris	11
Bankhead	4	Barnett	5	Grayston	38	Roberts	11
Castiglione	4	Daugherty	5	Dabbs	37	Ashmore	10
		Swartzman	5	Castiglione	36		

Notes: Box scores mising for the following games (line scores given—runs, hits, errors):

June 17	Siloam Springs	8 9 3	June 19	Siloam Springs	2 9 0
	Neosho	4 7 5		Fayetteville	1 8 0
June 29	Fayetteville	7 7 3	June 30	Neosho	10 11 3
	Siloam Springs	0 5 3		Fayetteville	8 13 6

**The missing statistics may have affected leaders in doubles and, more importantly, batting average in the race between Fash and Arlitt, managers of Fayetteville and Carthage, respectively.*

****Ashmore played only 32 games at the beginning of the season. He appears to have dropped out of professional baseball forever.*

PITCHERS*

WINS		PCT		ERA*	
Playfair	9-1	Playfair	9-1 (.900)	Narieka	1.85**
Greble	9-3	Obenour	6-1 (.857)	Playfair	1.86
Prylich	9-3	Willey	7-2 (.777)	Obenour	1.98
Willey	7-2	Greble	9-3 (.750)	Prater	2.25
Prater	7-7	Prylich	9-3 (.750)	Nasalik	3.14
Obenour	6-1	Prater	7-7 (.500)	Rundas	3.22
Rundas	6-6	Rundas	6-6 (.500)	Prylich	3.44

IP		H***		SO***		BB***	
Prater	108	Obenour	41	Nasalik	119	Obenour	23
Prylich	102	Peterlich	49	Greble	97	Narieka	24
Bunch	100 2/3	Dothager	54	Playfair	91	Brown	31
Nasalik	92	Playfair	66	Brown	82	Peterlich	35
Playfair	92	Quante	67	Prylich	71	Byerly	37
Willey	89 2/3	Nasalik	68	Willey	71	Christy	37
Greble	89 1/3	Byerly	71	Prater	67	Playfair	41
Christy	81 2/3	Rundas	71	Christy	65	Greble	43
Henderson	79 2/3	Christy	79	Narieka	65	Prylich	63

*Notes: Because of missing box scores (see 1940 hitting leaders for specific games) and scoring lapses, earned runs are not listed and ERAs often include best guesses based on newspaper game summaries.

**From June 6 through June 28, his last 7 appearances of the season (26 1/3 innings), Narieka did not give up a single earned run.

***For hits and walks, only confirmed records are listed. For strikeouts, Prylich, Willey, and Prater were high enough to list even though strikeout statistics for one game for Prylich and Willey and two games for Prater were not available.

APPENDIX D
Arkansas State/Arkansas-Missouri League
Yearly All-Stars

1934 Arkansas State League All-Stars*[50]
*Final season. Mid-season All-Stars were not the same.

F—Fayetteville, SS—Siloam Springs,
B—Bentonville, R—Rogers

All-Stars
Parker Rushing, F	1B
Bill Homan, R	2B
Russell Mosier, SS	3B
David Bush, F-R	SS
John R. "Doc" Graves, SS	OF
Bill Beams, B	OF
Rudolf Woodrow, SS	OF
Bill Landthrip, SS	C
Clyde Glass, SS	Utility/CF (Manager)
Marvin Breuer, R	P
J.W. White, R	P
Pete Casey, R	Manager

Honorable Mention (Fayetteville)
Monty Johnson	2B
Douglas Scott (SS-R also)	OF
Allan Thomas	3B
Fred Hawn	C (Manager)
Thornton Buchanan	P
Paul Linch	P
Harold Ensley (B also)	OF
Frank Mathews	Manager

Notable Opponents:
Woody Fair, R	OF
Thurston Crutchfield, R	P
Kenneth Allum, SS	SS
Buck White, SS	P
Jim Nicely, B	1B
Herb Wollard, B	P

1935 Arkansas State League All-Stars*[51]

Final season. Mid-season All-Stars were not the same.

F—Fayetteville, SS—Siloam Springs, B—Bentonville,
R—Rogers, H—Huntsville, C—Cassville

All-Stars

Frank Stapleton, R	1B
Monty Johnson, F	2B
Doug White, F	3B
David Bush, R	SS
Howard Roberts, C	OF
Ben Turner, SS	OF
Rudolf Woodrow, SS	OF
Tom (Walker) Cooper, R	C
Les Wilson, F	Utility
Warren Fralich, F	P
George Gibson, B	P
Ray Powell, SS	Manager

Honorable Mention (Fayetteville)

Pete Ashmore	SS
Pete Negri	OF
Allan Thomas	3B-OF
Jim Jensen	P
Fred Cato	C (Manager)

Notable Opponents:

Wilbur Davis, B	1B (Manager)
Ace Villipique, B	OF
Kenneth Allum, SS	SS
Andy Sinay, SS	P
Bill Werner, H	C (Manager)
Howard Johnson, H	OF
Duane (Dee) Kratzer, C	2B
Woody Fair, C	SS
Ed Hawks, C	Manager
Cotton Hill, R	P
Al Gerhauser, R	P

1936 Arkansas-Missouri League All-Stars[52]

F—Fayetteville, SS—Siloam Springs, B—Bentonville,
R—Rogers, M—Monett, C—Cassville

All-Stars

Les Rock, B	1B
Al Klier, C	2B
Bob Ludwig, SS	3B
Mel Tonnsen, B	SS
Kermit Lewis, SS	LF
Rudolph "Woody" Tone, SS	CF*, **
Ace Villipique, B	RF
Johnny Dellasega, C	C
Andy Sinay, SS	Utility
Clint Raper, SS	RHP
Henry Davis, M	LHP
Ray Powell, SS	Manager*

Repeat All-Star from 1935
**Played under the name Rudolph Woodrow in 1934 and 1935, All-Star selection both years.*

Honorable Mention (Fayetteville)

Paul Fugit	1B
Doug White	3B
Pete Ashmore	SS
Barney Lutz	LF
Elmer Honea	CF
Fred Hawn	C (Manager)
Les Wilson	Utility
Earl Smalling	P

Notable Opponents:

Buzz Arlitt, M	1B (Manager)
Woody Fair, M	3B
Tony Sams, R	SS
Al Gerhauser, R	P
Gene McCarty, C	LF
Erwin "Zeke" Gansauer, C	P (Manager)
Steve Lokotas, B	2B
Homer "Doc" Ledbetter, B	RF (Manager)
Bill Werner, SS	C
Thurman "Joe E." Tucker, SS	RF

1937 Arkansas-Missouri League All-Stars[53]

F—Fayetteville, SS—Siloam Springs, B—Bentonville,
R—Rogers, M—Monett, C—Cassville, N—Neosho

All-Stars
Paul Fugit, F	1B
Gerry Priddy, R	2B
Bob McCarron, F	3B
Tony Sams, R	SS*
Arnold "Doc" Evans, N	LF
Floyd Hundley, SS	CF
Barney Lutz, F	RF*
Al Harvatin, SS	C
Ken Blackman, F	Utility/Catcher (Manager)
Loy Hanning, F	RHP
Claude Tarrant, N	LHP
Ted Mayer, R	Manager

Repeat All-Star from 1936
**Repeat All-Star from 1935 and 1936*

Honorable Mention (Fayetteville)
Jack Troupe	LF
Earl Naylor	CF
Ed Smith	P
Andy Sinay	P**
Fred Hawn	C (Manager)
Les Wilson	Utility
Earl Smalling	P

Notable Opponents:
Frank Milani, R	1B
Bill Burich, R	3B
Al Klier, N	2B*
Mel Tonnsen, N	SS*
Ray Kommy, N	LF
Pete Ashmore, SS	SS*
Ray Powell, SS	Manager*
Melvin Autry, M	C
Joe Davis, M	P (Manager)

1938 Arkansas-Missouri League All-Stars[54]
F—Fayetteville, SS—Siloam Springs, R—Rogers,
M—Monett, N—Neosho, C—Carthage

All-Stars

Cyril "Butch" Moran, R	1B
Steve Luby, N	2B
Ray Lawrence, C	3B
Florian Zielinski, N	SS
Frank DaLuga, C	LF
Earl Naylor, F	CF*
Ray Kommy, N	RF*
Dan Radokovich, N	C
Clifford "Bud" Knox, F	Utility/Catcher (Manager)
Bill Gill, N	RHP
Leon Skidgel, C	LHP
Denny Burns, N	Manager

*Repeat All-Star from 1937
**Repeat All-Star from 1936

Honorable Mention (Fayetteville)

Melvin Schwab	1B
Bill Seal	2B
Hans "Whitey" Kreuger	3B
Harry Williams	P
Charles Epps	P
Wes Carolan	RF
Earl "Inky" Watkins	LF
Les Wilson	Utility
Earl Smalling	P

Notable Opponents:

Adolf "Buzz" Arlitt, C	1B (Manager)
Charlie Knoblauch, C	2B
Irwin Knoblauch, C	SS
Mike Sertich, SS	C (Manager)
Clarence "Hooks" Iott, SS	P
Marv "Wimpy" Wolverton, R	3B
Augie Navarro, R	C
Harry "Hal" Toomes, R	P
Erwin "Erv" Dusak, M	CF
Joe Sileber, N	RF
Ansel Owen, N	LF

1939 Arkansas-Missouri League All-Stars[55]
F—Fayetteville, M—Monett, N—Neosho, C—Carthage

All-Stars
Adolf "Buzz" Arlitt, C	1B**
Frank Oceak, F	2B (Manager)
Grant Harris, C	3B
Ed Checkley, F	SS
Ansel Owen, N	LF*
Bill Sarver, N	CF
Harvey Beaster, C	RF
"Elmer" Ralph Houk, N	C
Clarence "Ripper" Collins, F	Utility
George Bender, F	RHP
Francis "Hank" Henry, M	LHP
Denny Burns, N	Manager*

Repeat All-Star from 1938
Repeat All-Star from 1936 and 1938

Honorable Mention (Fayetteville)
Ken Grosse	1B
Harry Hatch	3B
Ray Parrott	CF
Joe Szuch	RF
Rudy Briner	C
Clifford Stebe	P

Notable Opponents:
Jim Paul, N	1B
Charlie Knoblauch, N*	2B
Steve Greble, N	RF
Mike Sakovich, M	3B
Fred Hawn, M	Manager (C)
Frank DaLuga, C*	2B
John Pavlich, C	C
Roman Deller, C	P

1940 Arkansas-Missouri League All-Stars[56]
F—Fayetteville, M—Monett, N—Neosho, C—Carthage

Arkansas All-Stars

Charles "Herb" Fash, F	1B (Manager)
Joe "Red" Cornella, F	2B
Glenn Calloway, F	3B
"Chief" Frisco Roberts, SS	SS
Herb Moore, SS	LF (Manager)
Alton Swartzman, SS	CF
Dale Myers, SS	RF
Bill "Whitey" Johnson, F	C
Caesar "Skee" Russo, F	Utility
"Farmer" Joe Prylich, F	P
Earl Dothager, SS	P

Repeat All-Star from 1939
**Repeat All-Star from 1936, 1938, and 1939*

Missouri All-Stars

Adolf "Buzz" Arlitt, C**	1B (Manager)
Eddie Barnett, C	2B
Grant Harris, C	3B
Don Wiegand, N	SS
Charley Gibson, C	LF
Lloyd Peterson, C	CF
Charley Amsberg, N	RF
Rex Twibell, N	C
Pete Castiglione, C	Utility
Bob Playfair, C	P
Walt Nasalik, N	P

APPENDIX E
Arkansas State/Arkansas-Missouri League All Time Records

Single Season Records—Batting

Batting Average
.397, Duane "Dee" Kratzer, Cassville, 1935
.392, Cyril "Butch" Moran, Rogers, 1938
.387, John R. "Doc" Graves, Siloam Springs, 1934 (short season)
.386, Monty Johnson, Fayetteville, 1935
.385, Arnold "Doc" Evans, Neosho, 1937
.374, Clyde Glass, Siloam Springs, 1934 (short season)
.374, Paul Fugit, Fayetteville, 1937

Home Runs
28, Kermit Lewis, Siloam Springs, 1936
24, Steve Greble, Neosho, 1939
22, Cyril "Butch" Moran, Rogers, 1938
21, Woody Fair, Cassville-Monett, 1936
21, Howard Roberts, Cassville, 1935

RBIs
132, Adolph "Buzz" Arlitt, Carthage, 1938
125, Rudolph "Woody" Tone, Siloam Springs, 1936
114, Cyril "Butch" Moran, Rogers, 1938
106, Adolph "Buzz" Arlitt, Carthage, 1939
99, Tony Sams, Rogers, 1937

Hits
183, Paul Fugit, Fayetteville, 1937
171, Harvey Beaster, Carthage, 1939
164, Kermit Lewis, Siloam Springs, 1936
160, Marv "Wimpy" Wolverton, Rogers, 1938
159, Cyril "Butch" Moran, Rogers, 1938

Runs
130, Kermit Lewis, Siloam Springs, 1936
129, Steve Greble, Neosho, 1939
127, Steve Luby, Neosho, 1938
124, Cliff VanSickel, Monett, 1938
120, Marv "Wimpy" Wolverton, Rogers, 1938

2Bs
43, Cyril "Butch" Moran, Rogers, 1938
40, Bill Sarver, Neosho, 1939
38, Barney Lutz, Fayetteville, 1937
37, Harvey Beaster, Carthage, 1939
35, Marv "Wimpy" Wolverton, Rogers, 1938
35, Paul Fugit, Fayetteville, 1937

3Bs
16, Hans "Whitey" Kreuger, Fayetteville, 1938
14, Lindy Serpa, Rogers, 1938
14, Al Klier, Cassville, 1936
14, Ben Turner, Siloam Springs, 1935
13, six players tied

SBs
76, Steve Luby, Neosho, 1938
55, Ansel Owen, Neosho, 1938
48, Bill Sarver, Neosho, 1939
45, Rudolph "Woody" Tone, Siloam Springs, 1936
44, Ansel Owen, Neosho, 1939

Single Season Records—Batting

Wins
3, Clint Raper, Siloam Springs, 1936
20, Bill Gill, Neosho, 1938
20, George Bender, Fayetteville, 1939
19, Ray Strunk, Bentonville, 1936
19, W. Harrel "Hal" Toenes, Rogers, 1938
19, Denny Horton, Neosho, 1939

Winning Percentage
.900 (9-1), Bob Playfair, Carthage, 1940 (Half season)
.889 (8-1), Everett Hill, Siloam Springs, 1934 (Short season)
.870 (20-3), Bill Gill, Neosho, 1938
.864 (11-2), Johnny (Al) Murray, Siloam Springs, 1935

.857 (6-1), Jim Obenour, Carthage, 1940 (Half season)

IPs
255, Erwin "Zeke" Gansauer, Cassville, 1936
249, Clint Raper, Siloam Springs, 1936
249, W. Harrel "Hal" Toenes, Rogers, 1938
231, Robert Olson, Fayetteville, 1936
231, Ray Clark, Rogers, 1936
229, Erwin "Zeke" Gansauer, Cassville, 1935

SOs
266, Bill Gill, Neosho, 1938
230, Leon Skidgel, Carthage, 1938
208, George Bender, Fayetteville, 1939
197, Tom Lally, Carthage, 1939
195, W. Harrel "Hal" Toenes, Rogers, 1938

CG
24, George Bender, Fayetteville, 1939
22, W. Harrel "Hal" Toenes, Rogers 1938
21, Tom Lally, Carthage, 1939
21, Eli Peterlich, Neosho, 1939
21, Bill Gill, Neosho, 1938

ERA
1.35, Johnny (Al) Murray, Siloam Springs, 1936
1.63, Loy Hanning, Fayetteville, 1937
1.85, Joe Narieka, Carthage, 1940 (Half season)
1.86, Bob Playfair, Carthage, 1940 (Half season)
1.98, Jim Obenour, Carthage, 1940 (Half season)
2.06, Clint Raper, Siloam Springs, 1936

Game/Consecutive Records

Consecutive Games Hitting Streak:
27, Ken Grosse, Fayetteville, ending 7/10/1939
25, Duane "Dee" Kratzer, Cassville, ending 8/13/1935

Consecutive Hits:
9, Cyril "Butch" Moran, Rogers, over 3 games, ending 7/15/1938

Hits in a Doubleheader:
8, Pete Ashmore, Fayetteville (vs. Monett), 6/21/1936, 8 for 8

Consecutive Home Runs:
4, Adolph "Buzz" Arlitt, Carthage (vs. Monett), 5/14/1939, doubleheader

Home Runs, Consecutive Innings:
3, Bobby Neighbors, Siloam Springs (vs. Bentonville), 6/22/1936

Home Runs in Single Game (Team):
10, Fayetteville (vs. Siloam Spring)s, doubleheader, 5/31/1938

RBIs (Game):
10, Pete Ashmore, Fayetteville (vs. Siloam Springs), 6/7/1940

Runs (Game):
6, Ken Grosse, Fayetteville (vs. Monett), 6/14/1939

Runs (Game)(Team):
28, Fayetteville (vs. Siloam Springs), 6/7/1940, 28-6
26, Fayetteville (vs. Monett), 6/14/1939, 26-5

Hits (Game)(Team):
25, Fayetteville (vs. Monett), 6/14/1939

Stolen Bases (Single Inning):
4, Ace Villipique (vs. Fayetteville), Bentonville, 8/28/1935

Stolen bases (Game)(Team):
15, Neosho (vs. Rogers), 6/4/1938

Stolen Bases (Team)(Season):
315, Neosho, 1938

Left on Base (Game)(Team):
17, Fayetteville (vs. Monett), 6/4/1938

Consecutive Wins (Pitcher):
10, Clint Raper, Siloam Springs, 1936
10, Cotton Hill, Rogers, 1935

Most Strikeouts (Game):
20, Kenneth Rutledge, Monett (vs. Carthage), 7/9/1938
18, Leon Skidgel, Carthage (vs. Neosho), 6/20/1938

Consecutive Wins (Team):
10, Siloam Springs, 1934 and 1936; Fayetteville, 1937

Double Plays (Game)(Team):
5, Fayetteville (vs. Neosho), 7/8/1937

Chances, OF, (Game):
9, Earl Naylor, Fayetteville (vs. Rogers), 7/19/1938

Errors, (Game)(Team):
10, Siloam Springs (vs. Carthage), 6/23/1938
9, Fayetteville (vs. Neosho), 6/23/1938

APPENDIX F
Arkansas State/Arkansas-Missouri League
No-Hitters

No Hitters

6/15/34: *Herb Wollard, Bentonville, 7-1, seven-inning win over Rogers*

7/4/37: *Walt Ward and LeRoy Youngblood, Monett, 1-0, seven-inning combined win at Siloam Springs*

8/15/38: *Howard Wagenhurst and Leon Skidgel, Carthage, 7-0, nine-inning combined home win over Rogers*

6/9/40: *Walt Nasalik, Neosho, 1-0, seven-inning loss at Fayetteville*

And Near No-Hitters

7/9/36: *Willard "Lefty" Hawkins, Fayetteville, seven innings of no-hit ball, lost 7-6 to Cassville*

8/7/38: *Ed Smith, Fayetteville, scheduled seven-inning game, no-hitter for seven, then eight innings, lost 1-0 on two-hitter to Rogers at home*

4/29/39: *George Bender, Fayetteville, 7 2/3 innings no-hitter against Carthage at home, won 1-0 on two-hitter*

5/9/40: *"Farmer" Joe Prylich, Fayetteville, wins 3-0 one-hitter at Siloam Springs, the only hit a disputed ground ball, Prylich walked 9, struck out 14*

APPENDIX G
Arkansas State/Arkansas-Missouri League Major Leaguers

ALTHOUGH IT WAS a small, backwater Class D minor league, the Arkansas State/Arkansas-Missouri League still produced a number of players who made it to the major leagues and it also included several who had been to the "big show" before coming down to the Ozarks later in their careers.

The following player summaries are divided into position players and pitchers, for those who made it to the majors after their Arkansas State/Arkansas-Missouri League experience, while the fellows who had already been to the big leagues, a smaller group, are lumped together.

Special mention is given to a handful of men who, while they never made it to the majors as players, either got there as coaches or scouts or in one case (Wilbur Davis) simply had one season so spectacular that he is included for that reason alone.

To The Majors: Position Players

Walker Cooper[57]
- ASL/AM-L: *1935, Rogers, First Team All-Star Catcher, Hit .359 with 14 HRs, 79 RBIs.*
- Major Leagues:
  - *18-year career, 1940-1957, 8 years with St.L.-N, 4 with NY-N*
  - *8-Time All-Star, .285 lifetime average with 1341 H, 73 HRs, 240 2B, 812 RBIs*
  - *Listed as one of the "400 Greatest" players of all time in Total Baseball.*

Mickey Owen[58]
- ASL/AM-L: *1934, Rogers/Bentonville, Catcher, Hit .228 with 1 HRs, 8 RBIs in 16 games*
- Major Leagues:
    - *13-year career, 1937-1954, 4 years with St.L.-N, 5 years with Brooklyn-N*
    - *4-Time All-Star, .255 lifetime average with 929 Hs, 14 HRs, 163 2Bs, 378 RBIs*

Erv Dusak[59]
- ASL/AM-L: *1938, Monett, Honorable Mention All-Star OF, Hit .351 with 18 HRs*
- Major Leagues:
    - *9-year career, 1941-1952, 7+ years with St.L.-N, 1+ years with Pitt-N*
    - *.243 lifetime average with 24 HRs, 106 RBIs; 0-3 as pitcher in 23 games, 54 IPs*

Ralph Houk[60]
- ASL/AM-L: *1939, Neosho, First Team All-Star Catcher Hit .286 with 56 RBIs, 27 SBs*
- Major Leagues:
    - *8-year career, 1947-1954, NY-A*
    - *.272 lifetime BA in 91 games with 158 ABs*
    - *20 year career as a manager, 1961-1984, 11 years in two tours with NY-A, also with Det-A and Boston-A*
    - *Won pennant and World Series in 1961 and 1962, first two years as manager, NY-A*

Sherm Lollar[61]
- ASL/AM-L: *1936-1939, Fayetteville, Bat Boy*
- Major Leagues:
    - *18-year career, 1946-1963 (1952-1963, Chi-A)*
    - *.264 lifetime BA with 1415 Hs, 155 HRs, 244 2Bs, 808 RBIs*

- *7-time All-Star, led AL catchers in fielding 1951, 1953, 1956, 1960, 1961 (.998 avg.)*
- *Won first three AL Gold Glove Awards for Catchers: 1957, 1958, 1959*
- *Major League Coach – 1964-1968 (Balt/Oak-A)[62] and Minor League Manager – 1973-1974[63]*
- *Listed as one of the "400 Greatest" players of all time in Total Baseball*

Earl Naylor
- ASL/AM-L: *1937-1938, Fayetteville, Honorable Mention All-Star (1937), First Team All-Star (1938), OF*
- Major Leagues:[64]
  - *3-year career, 1942-1943 (Phi-N), 1946 (Brooklyn-N)*
  - *.186 lifetime BA in 290 ABs, with 3 HRs, 28 RBIs*

Bob Neighbors
- ASL/AM-L: *1936-1937, Siloam Springs, Honorable Mention All-Star (1937), 2B*
- Major Leagues:[65]
  - *1-year career, 1939, St.L-A, SS*
  - *.182 BA in 7 G, 11 ABs, with 1 HRs, 1 RBIs*
  - *Missing in Action (MIA) in N. Korea 1952*

Gerry Priddy
- ASL/AM-L: *1937, Rogers, First Team All-Star, 2B*
- Major Leagues:[66]
  - *11-year career, 1941-1953, with four clubs (NY-, Wash-, St. L-, and Det-A)*
  - *.265 lifetime BA, with 4720 ABs, 1252 Hs, 232 2Bs, 61 HRs, 541 RBIs*

Les Rock
- ASL/A-ML: *1936, Bentonville, First Team All-Star, 1B*
  - *.333 BA led A-ML in batting, 1936, winning closest batting race in ASL/A-ML history. Promoted directly to the major leagues at season's end*
- Major Leagues:[67]
  - *1-year career, 1936, Chi-A*
  - *.000 BA in 2 G, with 1 ABs, 1 RBIs*

Pete Castiglione
- ASL/A-ML: *1940, Carthage, First Team All-Star, Utility Hit .299 with 70Hs, 13 2Bs, 36 RBIs*
- Major Leagues:[68]
  - *8-year career, 1947-1953, Pittsburgh; 1953-1954, St. L.-N*
  - *.255 BA in 545 G, with 426 Hs, 62 2Bs, 24 HRs, 150 RBIs*

To The Majors: Pitchers

Marvin Breuer
- ASL/A-ML: *1934, Rogers, Pitcher, 9-9 record*
- Major Leagues:[69]
  - *5-year career, 1939-1943, NY-A*
  - *25-26 lifetime Won-Loss record in 86 G, with 60 GS, 23 CG, 484 IP, 226 SOs, 4.03 ERA*

Al Gerhauser
- ASL/A-ML: *1935 and 1936, Honorable Mention All-Star (1935-1936), Rogers, P*
- Major Leagues:[70]
  - *5-year career, Phi-N, Pit-N, St. L.-A*
  - *25-50 lifetime Won-Loss record, 149 G, 79 GS, 27 CGs, 643 IPs, 4.13 ERA*

Loy Hanning
- ASL/A-ML: 1937, *Fayetteville, First Team All-Star, Right-handed Pitcher*
- Major Leagues:[71]
    - *2-year career, 1939 and 1942, St. L.-A*
    - *1-2 lifetime Won-Loss record in 15 G, with 1 GS, 27 IPs, 6.26 ERA*

Clarence "Hooks" Iott
- ASL/A-ML: *1938, Siloam Springs, Honorable Mention All-Star, Pitcher*
- Major Leagues:[72]
    - *2-year career, 1941 and 1947 (St.L-A and NY-N)*
    - *3-9 lifetime Won-Loss record in 26 G, with 9 GS, 2 CGs, 81 IPs, 7.05 ERA*

Walter I. "Jumbo" Brown
- ASL/A-ML: *1935, Bentonville, Pitcher*
- Major Leagues:[73]
    - *1-year career, 1947, St. L.-A*
    - *Lifetime record in 19 G, with 46 IPs, 4.89 ERA*

From the Majors: Before the ASL/A-ML

Clarence "Heinie" Mueller
- ASL/A-ML: *1938, Monett, Manager*
- Major Leagues:[74]
    - *11-year career, 1920-1929, 1935 (St. L.-N, NY-N, Bos-N, St. L-A)*
    - *.282 lifetime average in 693 G, with 2118 ABs, 597 Hs, 87 2Bs, 37 3Bs, 22 HRs, 272 RBIs*

Ray "Rabbit" Powell
- ASL/A-ML: *1935-1936, Siloam Springs, Manager, All-Star Manager (1935-1936)*

- Major Leagues:[75]
    - 9-year career, 1913 (Det-A), 1917-1924 (Bos-N)
    - .268 lifetime average in 875 G, with 3324 AB, 890 Hs, 117 2Bs, 67 3Bs, 35 HRs, 276 RBIs
    - Played centerfield for the Boston Braves on May 1, 1920 in what at the time was the longest major league game in history, a 26-inning 1-1 tie between the Braves and the Brooklyn Dodgers.[76]

Frank Sigafoos
- ASL/A-ML: *1938, Monett, Manager*
- Major Leagues:[77]
    - 3-year career – 1926 (Phi-A), 1929 (Det- and Chi-A), 1931 (Cin-N)
    - .201 lifetime average in 55 G, with 134 ABs, 27 Hs, 3 2Bs, 13 RBIs

Denny Burns
- ASL/A-ML: *1937-1939, Neosho, Manager/P (1937 – Honorable Mention All-Star, P; 1938 and 1939 All-Star Manager)*
- Major Leagues:[78]
    - 2-year career, 1923-1924, Phi-A
    - 8-9 lifetime Won-Loss record in 41 G, with 20 GS, 9 CGs, 181 IPs, 4.62 ERA

Ed Hawk(s)
- ASL/A-ML: *1934, Rogers/Bentonville, 1935, Cassville, Manager*
    - Helped form the Arkansas State League
- Major Leagues:[79]
    - 1-year career, 1911, St. L-A
    - 0-4 lifetime Won-Loss record in 5 G, with 4 GS, 4 CGs, 37 IPs, 3.35 ERA

Special Mention

Fred Hawn
- ASL/A-ML: *1934, 1936-1937, Fayetteville, 1939, Monett, Manager/Catcher*
  - *1934 and 1935* – Honorable Mention All-Star
  - *From Fayetteville (born in Huntsville)*
- Major Leagues:[80]
  - *27-year career as a scout for St.L-N. Signed 22 players who made it to the major leagues, including: Wally Moon (1954 N.L. Rookie of the Year), Hal Smith, Lindy McDaniel, Von McDaniel, Mel McGaha, Jim Beauchamp, and Jim King.*

Frank Oceak
- ASL/ A-ML: *1939, Fayetteville, Manager/IF, First Team All-Star, 2B*
  - *1939 – .310 average in 107 G, with 122 Hs, 20 2Bs, 4 3Bs, 18 SBs, 66 RBIs*
  - *Managed only Fayetteville champions – won the league pennant both halves of the 1939 split season*
- Major Leagues:[81]
  - *11-year career as a coach, 1958-1964 Pit-N, 1965 Cin-N, 1970-1972 Pit-N*

Wilbur "Cordwood" Davis
- ASL/A-ML: *1935, Bentonville, Manager/IF, Honorable Mention All-Star, 1B*
  - *1935 – .354 average in 105 G, with 146 Hs, 20 2Bs, 5 3Bs, 12 HRs, 14 SBs, 93 RBIs*
  - *Struck out only 17 times in 412 official ABs*
- Minor Leagues:
  - *1924 – Okmulgee, OK, Class C Western Association*[82]
  - *.400 BA, 260 Hs, 190 RBIs, 51 HRs*

APPENDIX H
Fayetteville Yearly Leaders

1934 Final Statistics—Fayetteville Educators[83]

Hitting *(20 Games or More)*

Player	G	AB	R	H	2B	3B	HR	RBI	SB	AVG
Norton	22	48	8	13	4	2	2	10	1	.330
Linch	22	53	7	17	3	1	—	7	2	.321
Poole, R	22	56	7	18	—	1	1	8	—	.321
Rushing	74	299	51	96	17	8	9	55	9	.321
Watson	58	213	40	62	13	6	3	32	5	.290
Thomas	68	271	39	76	11	4	0	38	8	.280
Buchanan	34	84	18	23	1	2	0	4	1	.273
Wilson	21	79	13	20	3	3	0	12	4	.253
Johnson	66	252	48	61	10	4	5	29	8	.242
Robello	26	50	10	12	5	—	1	7	1	.240
Hawn	65	228	26	51	6	3	0	32	2	.224

Parker Rushing led team in every hiting category.

Pitching *(First year statistics for pitching were very limited)*

Player	W	L	PCT
Robello	9	6	.600
Poole, R.	6	6	.500
Linch	6	7	.461
Buchanan	10	14	.417
Bolding	1	3	.250
Drake	0	3	.000

1935 Final Statistics—Fayetteville Bears[84]

Hitting *(20 Games or More)*

Player	G	AB	R	H	2B	3B	HR	RBI	SB	AVG
Johnson	78	316	72	122	23	13	9	64	9	.386
Casey*	59	180	31	62	14	3	2	45	2	.344
Thomas	87	353	79	120	17	4	2	43	19	.340
Wilson	48	172	25	57	15	3	2	29	3	.331
White	94	380	76	120	23	7	6	59	8	.316
Frederick	31	119	27	37	6	7	3	30	2	.311
Rushing	41	152	20	45	9	1	3	26	3	.296
Ashmore	68	285	43	81	16	1	4	40	9	.284
Cato*	92	312	64	87	16	5	4	56	6	.279
Negri	96	383	64	105	15	9	3	49	14	.274
Fralick	46	130	20	35	3	4	2	26	3	.269
Rucker	31	92	16	24	7	2	—	19	—	.261
Linch	23	52	10	13	4	1	—	8	1	.250
Murray	28	102	14	21	2	3	—	13	—	.206
Radabaugh	38	116	16	19	1	—	—	11	1	.163

Pitching *(10 Games or More)*

Player	G	W	L	PCT	ERA	CG	IP	SO	BB
Fralick	20	13	6	.684	3.37	17	172	124	32
Linch	17	6	6	.500	4.95	4	95	82	40
Rorie	23	6	7	.462	5.21	3	119	45	47
Rinckey	16	4	7	.364	4.86	8	105	31	37
Jensen	16	2	8	.200	5.70	5	100	82	74

1936 Final Statistics—Fayetteville Bears[85]

Hitting *(20 Games or More)*

Player	G	AB	R	H	2B	3B	HR	RBI	SB	AVG
Bohl	26	106	20	37	8	1	–	17	–	.349
White	111	442	76	145	22	6	13	81	3	.328
Lutz	119	479	81	155	27	10	3	64	6	.322
Wilson	120	477	84	143	19	6	5	63	8	.300
Fugit	94	357	43	105	18	4	3	39	4	.294
Ashmore	115	450	82	131	18	4	15	69	19	.291
Hawn	101	348	42	100	19	4	–	41	6	.288
Honea	117	449	70	128	18	4	20	86	10	.285
Bailey	40	162	19	45	9	4	1	17	5	.278
Bouyer	38	135	15	30	6	1	2	22	1	.222
Olson	48	111	8	24	5	–	–	7	–	.216
Perry	33	65	7	14	1	1	–	9	1	.216
Cross	34	78	4	13	1	–	–	4	–	.167
Smalling	25	75	3	8	–	–	1	3	–	.107

Pitching *(10 Games or More)*

Player	G	W	L	PCT	ERA	IP	SO	BB
Smalling	24	12	8	.600	3.00	178	96	68
Perry	28	7	5	.584	4.95	116	47	34
Olson	40	13	13	.500	3.80	231	163	80
Cross	32	9	13	.410	4.40	184	91	91
Lawson	15	2	6	.250	4.11	82	44	27

1937 Final Statistics—Fayetteville Angels[86]

Hitting *(20 Games or More)*

Player	G	AB	R	H	2B	3B	HR	RBI	SB	AVG
Fugit	125	489	80	183	35	5	5	85	10	.374
Lutz	125	472	83	158	38	5	5	81	18	.335
Blackman	116	376	78	124	10	8	7	72	18	.330
Troupe	121	469	74	143	26	13	0	55	12	.305
Naylor	90	351	47	106	20	6	5	65	10	.302
McCarron	125	479	96	139	18	8	1	46	11	.290
Cross	32	74	12	21	4	2	0	12	0	.284
Sinay	67	166	24	47	8	2	3	24	1	.283
Myer	120	409	74	102	21	4	11	70	8	.249
Poss	36	135	29	33	9	1	8	25	5	.244
Jarvis	56	231	40	54	9	2	3	15	2	.234
Hawn	44	111	10	25	6	0	0	11	1	.225
Hanning	33	80	9	18	3	0	1	4	0	.225
Nabor	69	259	38	55	9	0	3	27	6	.212
Smith	29	61	3	10	2	1	0	0	0	.164
Burse	32	72	2	8	1	0	0	4	0	.111

Pitching *(10 Games or More)**

Player	G	W	L	PCT	ERA	IP	SO	BB
Hannin	29	16	7	.696	1.63	181	144	28
Smith	28	10	9	.526	2.87	163	179	60
Cross	27	14	8	.636	2.93	180	113	44
Sinay	25	12	6	.667	3.42	171	65	44
Burse	31	10	11	.476	3.69	183	79	67

Buchanan was a perfect 5-0 with an ERA of 2.47, but only appeared in nine games for the season.

1938 Final Statistics—Fayetteville Angels[87]

Hitting *(20 Games or More)*

Player	G	AB	R	H	2B	3B	HR	RBI	SB	AVG
Seal	107	431	94	158	28	10	13	84	21	.367
Knox	100	371	73	121	28	1	17	84	14	.326
Naylor	97	379	85	121	23	8	19	94	24	.319
Schwab	119	481	92	151	32	4	14	80	10	.314
Young	47	217	33	66	15	4	5	36	3	.304
Kreuger	110	466	86	141	24	16	14	91	9	.303
Nowak	51	202	39	57	9	4	2	32	6	.282
Carolan	76	324	51	90	24	4	2	62	12	.278
Williams	37	90	20	24	3	3	1	14	0	.267
David	88	344	59	85	15	12	2	42	8	.247
Watkins	100	316	58	70	16	2	1	37	10	.222
Madden	48	178	44	39	3	2	1	15	9	.219
Boham	30	82	12	14	5	1	0	16	0	.171
Demster	59	151	21	24	4	2	1	13	1	.159
Heyne	31	69	6	11	2	0	0	8	0	.159
Epps	30	60	4	8	1	1	0	2	1	.133

Pitching *(10 Games or More)*

Player	G	W	L	PCT.	ERA	IP	SO	BB
Boham	29	16	5	.765	3.09	218	167	72
DeWoody	13	5	3	.625	5.95	65	32	24
Heyne	31	16	10	.615	3.42	210	153	61
Williams	29	12	11	.522	4.42	199	182	96
Epps	28	6	9	.400	5.45	132	160	166
Demster	24	6	10	.355	3.85	138	109	107

1939 Final Statistics—Fayetteville Angels[88]

Hitting *(20 Games or More)*

Player	G	AB	R	H	2B	3B	HR	RBI	SB	AVG
Hatch	111	404	100	138	30	3	4	74	19	.342
Parrott	54	212	49	71	11	3	3	43	2	.335
Grosse	109	465	115	155	24	5	0	55	30	.333
Odneal	33	97	16	31	9	1	1	17	2	.320
Oceak	107	393	82	122	20	4	0	66	18	.310
Szuch	118	501	107	155	31	7	8	90	13	.309
Bender	62	164	28	50	10	0	3	25	1	.305
Briner	109	417	76	123	25	1	5	76	11	.295
Checkley	115	425	82	122	24	7	5	69	12	.287
Litzinger	37	126	28	33	1	3	4	23	8	.262
Collins	90	313	53	81	16	5	6	55	4	.259
Bennett	79	295	50	76	10	3	6	46	7	.258
Young	45	181	35	46	4	3	2	23	8	.254
Stebe	29	82	11	20	1	0	2	8	0	.244
Barbolla	27	74	9	17	7	0	0	4	0	.230
Baker	22	82	12	14	6	0	1	6	2	.177
Smith	38	80	4	13	0	1	0	9	0	.163

Pitching *(10 Games or More)**

Player	G	W	L	PCT.	ERA	IP	SO	BB
Bender	26	20	4	.833	2.35	210	208	60
Stebe	29	17	9	.654	2.85	186	140	75
Barbolla	27	12	8	.600	4.09	178	134	75
Smith	37	14	12	.538	4.60	208	172	88
Odneal	27	13	6	.684	4.96	187	160	119

1940 Final Statistics—Fayetteville Angels[89]

Hitting*

Player	G	AB	R	H	2B	3B	HR	RBI	SB	AVG
Fash	44	153	30	56	18	3	4	35	8	.366
Calloway	34	123	8	41	5	0	0	16	7	.333
Ashmore	32	125	31	37	3	0	9	32	10	.296
Cornella	35	126	13	35	6	0	3	17	1	.278
Johnson	50	145	22	34	7	2	0	18	1	.234
Daugherty	48	165	27	35	4	6	5	31	3	.212
Russo	33	106	23	22	3	0	0	4	7	.208
Coppinger	11	33	5	6	3	0	0	2	1	.182
Luke	47	177	18	29	5	3	2	18	1	.164
Douglas	5	16	1	2	0	0	0	0	0	.125

Pitching*

Player	G	W	L	PCT	ERA	IP	H	SO	BB
Prylich	12	9	3	.750	3.44	102	89	71*	63
Prater	14	7	7	.500	2.25	108	84	67*	35*
Hines	6	2	3	.400	6.37	$35\ 1/3^*$	24*	29	47
Holl	10	2	7	.222	4.24	$76\ 2/3$	97	33	15
Schmedding	7	1	4	.200	2.75	$52\ 1/3$	47*	32*	13*

*1940 statistics for both batters and pitchers are problematic because box scores are missing for Fayetteville games of June 19, 29, and 30, and for pitchers because even with box scores some innings pitched, earned runs, hits, strikeouts, and walks totals are in doubt. Other pitching records are accurate.

END NOTES

1. *Fayetteville Daily Democrat (FDD)*, May 11, 1933. Unless otherwise specified, all subsequent references in the text to dates, advertisements, and classifieds, as well as all quotations and summaries, are from the *Fayetteville Daily Democrat* (or *Northwest Arkansas Times*). Specific articles and columns are referenced individually. Days and dates listed in the text are to the actual date a game or event occurred, unless noted otherwise.
2. "NAPBL (National Association of Professional Baseball Leagues) History," World Wide Web document, 1999, p. 1.
3. *The Encyclopedia of Minor League Baseball (EMLB)*, Lloyd Johnson and Miles Wolff, editors, second edition, Baseball, America, Inc., Durham, North Carolina, 1997, p. 11. The AAA classification, which became the highest level below the major leagues, was added in 1946. An A1 classification, between AA and A, existed from 1936 to 1945. Leagues with this classification were the Southern Association (1936 to 1945) and the Texas League (1936 to 1942). After World War II both of these leagues returned to AA classification. A Class E loop, the Twin Ports League existed for 19 games during the 1943 season. In 1963, all leagues below Class A were absorbed into Class A, and Rookie Leagues were added to develop younger, newer talent.
4. *FDD*, January 26, 1934, p. 4.
5. *The Fayetteville Angels or Why Baseball Is Our National Pastime being a History of the Arkansas-Missouri League*, Walter J. Lemke, Fayetteville, Arkansas, 1952, p. 29.
6. Information about the formation of the Arkansas State League is also thoroughly covered in *Depression Era Minor League Baseball:*

The Arkansas State League, 1934-1935 (Masters Thesis), Jeffrey John Aulgur, Hendrix College, Arkansas, 1986.

7. At least seven opening day starters for the Educators were holdovers from the 1933 Fayetteville All-Stars semi-pro team, including catcher and manager Freddie Hawn.
8. Early baseball records and reporting, especially of obscure minor leagues, oftentimes did not give the players' first names.
9. Things were going so well, the *Daily Democrat* reported, that when Freddie Hawn, Educators manager and catcher, finally got his first hit of the season in the second game of a double-header sweep at Siloam Springs, he kissed the base and shook hands with the Buffaloes' first baseman.
10. Bonnie and Clyde's criminal career touched Fayetteville at least three times. On June 23, 1933, two men, variously reported as Clyde and his brother Buck Barrow or as Buck and the gang's accomplice W. D. Jones (the more likely scenario), robbed R. L. Brown's Piggly Wiggly grocery store at 111 West Lafayette of between $20-$35 and escaped in Brown's delivery truck. During the robbers' getaway they killed Marshall H. D. Humphrey of Alma in a desperate shootout on south Highway 71 just north of Alma. In early 1934, shortly after busting fellow desperado Raymond Hamilton out of a Texas jail, the gang again passed through Fayetteville, this time picking up a stolen car before going on to Missouri. The last apparent local contact was either April 9 or 10, shortly after the gang had slain Commerce, Oklahoma Constable Cal Campbell, when they passed through town and came into possession of Washington County Clerk Merle Cruse's license plate: Arkansas 15-368.
11. *Majoring in the Minors: A History of the Kansas-Oklahoma-Missouri League*, John Hall, Oklahoma Bylines, Stillwater, Oklahoma, 1996, p. 4.
12. *Spalding Official Base Ball Guide* (1934), *The Sporting News*, St. Louis, 1935, p.247.
13. *Baseball, An Illustrated History*, based on a Documentary Filmscript by Geoffrey C. Ward and Ken Burns, Alfred Knopf, New York, 1994, p. 179.
14. *Total Baseball, The Official Encyclopedia of Major League Baseball (TB)*, John Thorn and Pete Palmer, editors, third edition, HarperPerennial, 1993, New York, p. 1153.
15. *EMLB*, p. 654.

16. Lemke, p. 15.
17. On Merchant's Days, local businesses bought up blocks of game tickets and offered them free of charge to their customers. It was always a good promotion and ensured better than usual crowds at the ballpark.
18. Lemke, p. 19.
19. *Madison County Record,* Huntsville, Arkansas, August 8, 1935, p. 1.
20. Lemke, p. 22.
21. Lemke, p. 10.
22. Cedar Rapids and Springfield belonged to the St. Louis Cardinals organization, Joplin and Kansas City to the New York Yankees.
23. Everyone seemed to have a nickname in 30s and "Red" Cross was one of the best. There were Docs, Chiefs, Cys, Jumbos, and so on. Some great names outside the ASL/AM-L were Ed "Bear Tracks" Greer, Cecil "Turkey" Tyson, Walter "Teapot" Frye, and Leo "Muscle" Shoals. In the ASL/AM-L, besides Red Cross, was Clarence "Hooks" Iott and perhaps the best of them all: Thornton "Hornbuckle Buck" Buchanan.
24. Lemke, pp. 2-3.
25. Martha Estes, Interview with Robert Henry, June 26, 2000. Lemke, p. 18, lists the schedule makers as Jim and Ora Bohart and Robert Henry, but Mr. Henry recalled it was Bernal Seamster who helped him create the difficult 5-team league schedule.
26. *Northwest Arkansas Times* (NWAT), July 8, 1937.
27. On April 1, 1938 the *Northwest Arkansas Times* listed all the players made free agents by Judge Landis. Among these were current Fayetteville players Dick Burse, Elmer Poss, Andy Sinay, Ken Blackman and Earl Naylor. Former Fayetteville players having moved up to Cedar Rapids, Iowa who were given free agency included Paul Fugit, Loy Hanning, Bob McCarron, Ken Meyer, Robert Olson and Doug White. Kenyon "Red" Cross and Barney Lutz formerly of Fayetteville and then with Decatur, Illinois were also freed by the Landis decision.
28. Lemke, "Angel Food" column, *NWAT,* May 2, 1938.
29. Other prizes included $1 in trade from H. L. Tuck Super Service to the player's favorite cafe and one-half gallon of Ward's Ice Cream to the Angel who first stole a base. The Monarch Eat Shop on East Center Street offered a free sandwich and drink to each Angels player and their manager after the team won its first game.

30. White almost immediately left Fayetteville, leaving June 19 to join Sioux City, Iowa in the Nebraska State League.
31. Lemke, "Angel Food" column, *NWAT,* July 5, 1938.
32. *Backwoods Baron: The Life Story of Claude Albert Fuller,* Frank L. Beals, Morton Publishing Company, Wheaton, Illinois, 1951, pp. 104-106. Despite his sponsorship of Arkansas-Missouri League games, Mr. Fuller, a five-term U.S. Congressman from Arkansas' Third Congressional District, lost the 1938 election to Clyde T. Ellis by the narrow margin of 37 votes.
33. Fayetteville attendance actually dropped in 1938 (from a reported 19,950 in 1937 to 13,850) but good crowds in Neosho and especially in Carthage, which had 35,000 paid customers for the year, boosted league attendance (records of which are not well documented) to probable record levels.
34. John Thorn, Pete Palmer, et. al., editors, *Total Baseball, The Official Encyclopedia of Major League Baseball,* sixth edition, Total Sports, New York, New York, 1999, p. 2463.
35. Carthage Business Manager George Rush made the motion to move the Monett franchise; and although the paper did not specify the one "against" vote, it seems fairly safe to assume that Monett did not vote to give up their own franchise.
36. Managers for the other Arkansas-Missouri League clubs in 1940 were: Buzz Arlitt, Carthage; Ed Grayston, Neosho; and Herb Moore, Siloam Springs.
37. Despite the name "Wings" on their new uniforms, the Angels did not change the name this time as they had four years before when they had so unceremoniously and rather comically become the Angels.
38. Later Times bus schedules simply listed the pick-up locations as at the square and at Shulertown. Shulertown, named for former University of Arkansas student and local entrepreneur Fred Shuler, referred to the "lower West Dickson" area. *Fayetteville: A Pictorial History,* Donning Company/Publishers, Norfolk-Virginia Beach, Virginia, 1982, p. 40.
39. *The Carthage Democrat,* Carthage, Missouri, June 30, 1940, p. 4, listed this score as Rogers over Siloam Springs 7-0.
40. Fayetteville manager Herb Fash and pitcher Joe Prylich went to Olean of the Class D Pony League while fellow Angels Glenn Calloway, Caesar "Skee" Russo, Bill "Whitey" Johnson, and Ralph

Prater caught on at Newport of the Class D Northeast Arkansas League. Carthage pilot Adolf "Buzz" Arlitt and six of his players, including Pete Castiglione and Jim Skidgel, were promoted to Hutchinson, Kansas of the Class C Western Association where Arlitt would continue his managerial duties.

41. "Anguish in the Ozarks When Arky-Missouri Folds," *The Sporting News,* July 25, 1940, p. 3. To provide Fayetteville with $2000 to stay in operation the other three teams of the league offered $500 each if the Dodgers would give just $500 themselves to save their farm team. Dodgers General Manager MacPhail declined to do so.
42. Lemke, p. 4.
43. *Spalding Official Base Ball Guide* (1934), *The Sporting News,* St. Louis, 1935, pp. 248-250.
44. *Spalding Official Base Ball Guide* (1935), *The Sporting News,* St. Louis, 1936, pp. 276-277, 279 and *FDD,* September 21, 1935.
45. *Spalding Official Base Ball Guide* (1936), *The Sporting News,* St. Louis, 1937, pp. 256-257, 259 and *FDD,* September 19, 1936.
46. *Spalding Official Base Ball Guide* (1937), *The Sporting News,* St. Louis, 1938, pp. 275-278 and *NWAT,* September 4, 1937.
47. *Spalding Official Base Ball Guide* (1938), *The Sporting News,* St. Louis, 1939, pp. 312-314, 316 and *NWAT,* September 10, 1938.
48. *Spalding Official Base Ball Guide* (1939), *The Sporting News,* St. Louis, 1940, pp. 336-337, 339 and *NWAT,* September 9, 1939.
49. *NWAT,* June 15, 1940; *Carthage Evening Press* and *Carthage Democrat,* June 22-July 1, 1940; and *Neosho Daily Democrat,* June 22-July 1, 1940.
50. *Spalding Official Base Ball Guide* (1934), *The Sporting News,* St. Louis, 1935, p.248.
51. *Spalding Official Base Ball Guide* (1935), *The Sporting News,* St. Louis, 1936, p. 275 and *FDD,* August 29, 1935.
52. *Spalding Official Base Ball Guide* (1936), *The Sporting News,* St. Louis, 1937, p. 256 and *FDD,* August 26, 1936.
53. *Spalding Official Base Ball Guide* (1937), *The Sporting News,* St. Louis, 1938, p. 275 and *NWAT,* August 21, 1937.
54. *Spalding Official Base Ball Guide* (1938), *The Sporting News,* St. Louis, 1939, p. 312.
55. *Spalding Official Base Ball Guide* (1939), *The Sporting News,* St. Louis, 1940, p. 336 and *NWAT,* August 28, 1939.

56. *NWAT,* June 27, 1940.
57. *TB,* p. 787.
58. *TB,* p. 1155.
59. *TB,* p. 837.
60. *TB,* p. 960.
61. *TB,* p. 1042.
62. *TB,* p. 2482.
63. *EMLB,* pp. 523, 527.
64. *TB,* p. 1131.
65. *TB,* p. 1132.
66. *TB,* p. 1184.
67. *TB,* p. 1213.
68. *TB,* p. 759.
69. *TB,* p. 1436.
70. *TB,* p. 1549.
71. *TB,* p. 1573.
72. *TB,* p. 1609.
73. *TB,* p. 1442.
74. *TB,* p. 1121.
75. *TB,* p. 1182.
76. *TB,* p. 2070.
77. *TB,* p. 1255.
78. *TB,* p. 1447.
79. *TB,* p. 1580.
80. *Tulsa World,* September 17, 1972.
81. *TB,* p. 2483.
82. *EMLB,* pp. 236, 654.
83. *Spalding Official Base Ball Guide* (1934), *The Sporting News,* St. Louis, 1935, pp. 248-250.
84. *Spalding Official Base Ball Guide* (1935), *The Sporting News,* St. Louis, 1936, pp. 276-277, 279 and *FDD,* September 21, 1935.
85. *Spalding Official Base Ball Guide* (1936), *The Sporting News,* St. Louis, 1937, pp. 256-257, 259 and *FDD,* September 19, 1936.
86. *Spalding Official Base Ball Guide* (1937), *The Sporting News,* St. Louis, 1938, pp. 275-278 and *NWAT,* September 4, 1937.
87. *Spalding Official Base Ball Guide* (1938), *The Sporting News,* St. Louis, 1939, pp. 312-314, 316 and *NWAT,* September 10, 1938.
88. *Spalding Official Base Ball Guide* (1939), *The Sporting News,* St. Louis, 1940, pp. 336-337, 339 and *NWAT,* September 9, 1939.

89. *NWAT,* June 15, 1940; *Carthage Evening Press* and *Carthage Democrat,* June 22-July 1, 1940; and *Neosho Daily Democrat,* June 22-July 1, 1940.

BIBLIOGRAPHY

Newspapers

Fayetteville Daily Democrat, Fayetteville, Arkansas, 1933-1937.
Northwest Arkansas Times, Fayetteville, Arkansas, 1937-1941.
Madison County Record, Huntsville, Arkansas, 1935.
Benton County Record and Democrat, Bentonville, Arkansas, 1934-1935.
Southwest Times Record, Fort Smith, Arkansas, 1940
The Carthage Evening Press, Carthage, Missour, 1940
The Carthage Democrat, Carthage, Missouri, 1940
The Neosho Daily Democrat, Neosho, Missouri, 1940
Joplin Globe, Joplin, Missouri, 1940
Springfield Daily News, Springfield, Missouri, 1940

Citations

American Decades, 1930-1939.
Aulgur, Jeffrey John, *Depression Era Minor League Baseball: The Arkansas State League, 1934-1935,* Masters Thesis, University of Arkansas, 1986.
Beals, Frank L., *Backwoods Baron: The Life Story of Claude Albert Fuller,* Morton Publishing Company, Wheaton, Illinois, 1951, pp. 104-106.
Berlage, Ingham, *Women in Baseball,* p. 83.
Burns, Ken and Ward, Geoffrey C, *Baseball, An Illustrated History,* based on a Documentary Filmscript, Alfred Knopf, New York, 1994, p. 179.
Davids, L. Robert, editor, *Minor League Stars, Vol. II, Cooperstown: Society for American Baseball Research* (SABR), 1985.
Davids, L. Robert, editor, *Minor League Stars, Vol. III, Cooperstown: Society for American Baseball Research* (SABR), 1992.

Doyle, Pat, Old-Time Baseball Database, 1999.

Dunlap, Buster, Interview, 1999.

Hall, John, *Majoring in the Minors: A History of the Kansas-Oklahoma-Missouri (K-O-M) League,* Oklahoma Bylines, Stillwater, Oklahoma, 1996, pp. 1-20.

Hawn, Maude (Mrs. Fred), Interview (Martha Estes), 1999.

Henry, Robert, Interviews (Martha Estes), 1999.

Jackson, Jerry, Managerial Lists for Arkansas State/Arkansas-Missouri League.

Johnson, Lloyd and Wolff, Miles, editors, *The Encyclopedia of Minor League Baseball,* second edition, Baseball America, Inc., Durham (NC), 1997.

Lemke, Walter J., *The Fayetteville Angels or Why Baseball Is Our National Pastime being A History of the Arkansas-Missouri League,* Fayetteville, Arkansas, 1952.

"NAPBL (National Association of Professional Baseball Leagues) History," World Wide Web document, 1999, p. 1.

Pietrusza, David, *Minor Miracles: The Legend and the Lore of Minor League Baseball.*

Schiefer, Carl L., *Washington County, Arkansas: A Geography of Population Change,* 1976.

Siroonian, Heather, "The Fayetteville Angels," Washington County Historical Society, *Flashback,* 1985, pp. 26-28.

Spalding Official Base Ball Guide, The Sporting News, St. Louis (MO), 1934, pp. 247-250.

Spalding Official Base Ball Guide, The Sporting News, St. Louis (MO), 1935, pp. 275-279.

Spalding Official Base Ball Guide, The Sporting News, St. Louis (MO), 1936, pp. 255-259.

Spalding Official Base Ball Guide, The Sporting News, St. Louis (MO), 1937, pp. 274-278.

Spalding Official Base Ball Guide, The Sporting News, St. Louis (MO), 1938, pp. 311-316.

Spalding Official Base Ball Guide — Reach, The Sporting News, St. Louis (MO), 1939, pp. 335-339.

Thorn, John and Palmer, Pete, editors, *Total Baseball,* third edition, Harper-Perennial 1993.

Thorn, John and Silverman, M., editors, *The Official Encyclopedia of Major League Baseball.*

U.S. Department of Interior Census Office, Sixteenth Census of the United States, 1940.

Washington County Office of Archives and Research Management, *Good Government League Papers,* 1933-1936, University of Arkansas Mullins Library, Special Collections, Fayetteville, Arkansas.

WPA Guide to 1930s Arkansas, 1941.

INDEX

Allum, Kenneth, 10, 151, 152
Alma (AR): 184
American Association: 40, 42
Amsberg, Charley:157
Arkansas State League: 3, 5, 8, 11, 18, 21, 25, 31, 33, 35, 40, 44, 74, 128, 135, 136, 138, 140, 142, 144, 146, 151, 152
Arkansas-Missouri League: 3, 43, 44, 46, 56, 58, 59, 60, 61, 62, 68, 69, 70, 73, 74, 75, 77, 78, 82, 88, 90, 92, 96, 99, 100, 102, 105, 107, 108, 109, 115, 116, 117, 119, 120, 121, 128, 129, 153, 154, 155, 156, 157, 167, 186
Arlitt, Adolf "Buzz": 45, 52, 56, 75, 81, 86, 94, 122, 129, 146, 153, 155, 156, 157, 159, 162, 186, 187
Ashmore, Pete: 28, 30, 33, 44, 46, 49, 54, 82, 110, 111, 112, 114, 146, 152, 153, 154, 161, 162
Aulgur, Jeffrey John: 184
Autry, Melvin: 71, 154
Baer, Max: vi, 13
Baggett, Bill: 40
Barnett, Eddie: 157
Barr, George: 42

Barrett, Charlie: 99
Barrow, Buck: 184
Barrow, Clyde: 11
Bauer, John "Angel": 111
Beams, Bill: 19, 151
Beasley, Sam; 11
Beaster, Harvey: 93, 98, 105, 156, 159, 160
Beck, Arlie: 21
Becker, Joe: 4
Bell, Carl: 114
Bender, George: 92, 98, 99, 100, 101, 102, 104, 105, 156, 160, 161, 165
Bengough, Benny: 44
Bennett, Bob: 100
Bentonville Mustangs: 45, 48, 54, 127, 128
Bentonville Officeholders: 8, 16, 25, 32, 127, 128
Bentonville White Sox: 25, 42
Berra, Yogi: 94
Berryville (AR): 21
Blackman, Ken: 52, 67, 69, 70, 128, 129, 154, 185
Blake, Betty: 35
Bogart, R. D.: 40
Bohart, Jim: 41, 60, 73, 88, 90, 98, 108, 115, 185

Bohl, Richard "Dick": 53
Bolding, Mack: 16, 34
Boston Braves: 22, 168, 172
Bramham, Judge William G.: 11, 17, 109
Breuer, Marvin: 13, 19, 151, 170
Briner, Rudy: 91, 93, 104, 156
Brooklyn Dodgers: 4, 11, 22, 108, 109, 110, 114, 116, 119, 129, 168, 169, 172,
Brooks, Kenneth: 23
Brown, Bob: 40
Brown, R. L.: 184
Brown, Walter I. "Jumbo": 184
Bryan, Leland: 40
Buchanan, Thornton "Hornbuckle Buck": 16, 52, 67, 86, 91, 151, 178, 185
Burich, Bill: 154
Burns, Denny: 75, 104, 129, 155, 156, 172, 184, 191
Burse, Dick: 65, 185
Bush, David "Dave": 7, 10, 12, 16, 151, 152
Bussy, Woodrow: 16
Buxton, Wallace: 40
Byrn, David: 26
Cain, Bill; 73, 87, 90, 95, 100, 108, 107
Calloway, Glenn: 116, 157, 186
Campbell, Constable Cal; 184
Carnes, Stubby: 14
Carolan, Wes: 155
Carthage Pirates: 73, 77, 78, 79, 80, 81, 83, 84, 85, 86, 87, 88, 89, 90, 91, 92, 93, 94, 95, 96, 97, 98, 99, 100, 101, 102, 103, 104, 105, 108, 111, 113, 114, 115, 117, 118, 127, 128, 131, 155, 156, 157, 159, 160, 161, 162, 163, 165
Casey, Maud: 68

Casey, Pete: 6, 20, 22, 23, 24, 29, 30, 53, 68, 128, 151
Cassville Blues: 46, 47, 48, 49, 51, 56, 59, 120, 143
Cassville Tigers: 24, 25, 26, 27, 29, 30, 31, 32, 33, 34, 35, 36, 127, 128
Castiglione, Pete: 157, 170, 187
Cato, Fred: 23. 30, 34, 128, 152
Cedar Rapids (IA): 43, 45, 59, 75, 80, 185
Chartrand, Maurice "Babe": 65, 67, 88
Checkley, Ed: 93, 104, 156
Chestnut, Art: 13
Chicago White Sox: 55
Cincinnati Reds: 53, 75, 128, 129
Clark, Ed: 86
Clark, J. O.: 5, 21, 39, 41, 73, 90, 116, 128
Clark, Ray: 161
Clay, Clifford: 48, 50
Clemmens, Jack; 23, 44, 47
Coker, Gary; 45, 47, 48, 128
Collins, Clarence "Ripper": 92, 103, 104, 156
Cooper, Mort: 29
Cooper, Walker ("Tom"): 28, 32, 33, 36, 44, 152, 167
Coppinger, John: 111
Cornella, Joe "Red": 115, 116, 157
Cotton States League: 52
Crawford, Charlie: 13
Cross, Kenyon "Red": 47, 48, 54, 71, 185
Crossley, "Cap": 43
Cruse, Merle: 11, 184
Crutchfield, Thurston: 151
Curtis, Leonard; 44
DaLuga, Frank; 155, 156
Daugherty, Mike: 111
David, Robert: 81

Davis, Cecil "Stormy": 22
Davis, Joe: 67, 129, 154
Davis, Wilbur "Cordwood": 22, 24, 128, 152, 167, 173
Day, Clifford: 128
Dayton Wings: 111, 113
Deberry, Hank: 76
Dellasega, Johnny: 153
Deller, Roman: 83, 86, 156
DeLuxe Eat Shop: 115
Detroit Tigers: 108
Doan, Ray: 20, 42
Dothager, Earl: 157
Drake, Jake: vii, 24, 53, 67
Duggans, Walter: 40
Dunlap, Buster: ii, vii, 7, 55, 71, 192
Dunlap, Frances "Sonny": 55, 68
Dusak, Erv: 81, 155, 168
Dyer, Eddie: 35
Earhart, Amelia: 63, 65
Eckert, Al G.: 20, 40
El Dorado Lions: 52
Ellis, Clyde T.: 186
Ensley, Harold: 13, 16, 151
Epps, Charles: 155
Estes, Martha: 11, 185, 192
Evangeline League: 67, 90
Evans, Arnold "Doc": 154, 159
Evans, John: 28, 33
Fair, Woody: 48, 56, 151, 152, 153, 159
Fairweather, Tom: 40
Fash, Charles "Herb": 110, 111, 112, 115, 116, 129, 146, 157, 186
Fayetteville Angels: 1, 7, 59, 61, 62, 63, 64, 65, 66, 67, 68, 69, 70, 71, 72, 75, 76, 77, 78, 79, 80, 81, 82, 83, 84, 85, 87, 88, 89, 90, 91, 92, 93, 94, 95, 96, 98, 99, 100, 101, 102, 103, 104, 105, 106, 108, 109, 110, 111, 112, 113, 114, 115, 119, 120, 121, 181, 183, 185, 186, 192
Fayetteville Bears: 20, 23, 24, 25, 26, 27, 28, 29, 30, 31, 32, 33, 34, 35, 36, 38, 40, 43, 44, 45, 46, 47, 48, 49, 50, 51, 52, 53, 54, 55, 56, 60, 61, 63, 93, 120, 128, 176, 177
Fayetteville Educators: 7, 8, 9, 10, 11, 12, 13, 14, 15, 16, 18, 19, 23, 52, 63, 120, 128, 175, 184
Fair Grounds ball park: iv, 6, 9, 10, 14, 15, 16, 17, 22, 29, 30, 32, 42, 43, 44, 45, 50, 51, 52, 53, 54, 55, 60, 63, 64, 66, 67, 68, 69, 70, 71, 76, 77, 78, 81, 83, 87, 89, 62, 94, 96, 98, 99, 101, 102, 105, 109, 111, 113, 114, 115
night baseball: 64, 65
Fayetteville All-Stars: vii, 184
Fayetteville Baseball Association: 40, 64
Fayetteville Daily Democrat: v, 23, 27, 42, 60, 66, 112, 183, 191
Fayetteville High School band: 25, 46, 110
Fields, Stroud: 44
Floyd, Pretty Boy: 20
Fort Smith Southwest-Times Record: 17
Fralich, Warren "Moose": 28, 29, 30, 33, 34, 35, 152
Frederick, Hal: 33, 34
Frye, Walter "Teapot": 185
Ft. Smith (AR): 76
Fugit, Paul: 44, 45, 46, 53, 54, 60, 62, 69, 153, 154, 159, 160, 185
Fulbright, J. W.: 107
Fulbright, Mrs. Roberta: vii
Fuller, Claude A.: 84, 186, 191

Futrall, J. C.: 106
Gansauer, Erwin "Zeke": 50, 57, 128, 153, 161
Garns, Randall: 14
Gehrig, Lou: 93
Georgia-Florida League: 47
Gerhauser, Al: 152, 153, 170
Gibson, Charley: 157
Gibson, George: 152
Gill, Bill: 83, 155, 160, 161
Giovanetti, Al: 111
Glass, Clyde: 6, 10, 19, 20, 128, 151, 159
Graves, John R. "Doc": 151, 159
Grayston, Ed: 129, 186
Greble, Steve: 104, 156, 159, 160
Greenhaw, Karl: 7
Greer, Ed "Bear Tracks": 185
Grosse, Ken: 91, 93, 96, 97, 99, 103, 104, 156, 164, 162
Hall, John: 184
Hamilton, Raymond: 184
Hanning, Loy: 69, 154, 161, 171, 185
Harris, Grant: 103, 156
Harris, Ralph: 77, 157
Harrison (AR): 6, 21
Harvatin, Al: 71, 154
Hatch, Harry: 92, 93, 103, 156
Hauger, Art: 42, 45, 128
Hauptmann, Bruno Richard: 38
Hawk(s), Ed: 3, 24, 25, 29, 128, 152, 172
Hawkins, Willard "Lefty": 43, 45, 52, 165
Hawn, Fred: ii, vi, vii, 4, 5, 6, 10, 13, 14, 15, 19, 35, 42, 43, 45, 46, 48, 49, 51, 54, 55, 60, 67, 74, 91, 128, 129, 151, 153, 154, 156, 173
Heerwagen, Louis M.: 10, 11
Henry, Francis "Hank": 156

Henry, Robert: 17, 21, 26, 73, 90, 92, 96, 100, 103, 106, 108, 109, 111, 116
Heyne, Rudy: 79, 81, 91
Hill, Cotton: 19, 33, 34, 54, 152, 162
Hill, Everett: 160
Hindenburg: 62
Hodgson, Mark: 65
Holmes, Howard "Ducky": 109, 114, 119
Homan, Bill: 19, 44, 151
Homesley, John Henry: 111
Honea, Elmer: 43, 44, 46, 47, 48, 51, 52, 54, 55, 153
Horton, Denny: 160
Hot Springs (AR): 20, 42, 49
Houk, Ralph: 94, 98, 156, 168
Howell, Van: 7
Hull, Cordell: 59
Humphrey, Marshall H. D.: 184
Hundley, Floyd: 154
Huntsville Red Birds: 24, 25, 26, 29, 30, 31, 32, 33, 34, 36, 40, 41, 128, 152
Iott, Clarence "Hooks": 155, 171, 185
Jackson, Judge Homer: 46
Jarvis, Dan: 62, 65
Jensen, Jim: 31, 44, 152
John, Johnny: 31, 32
Johnnie Porter: 17
Johnson, Bill "Whitey": 111, 116, 157, 186
Johnson, Howard: 152
Johnson, Monroe "Monty": 10, 26, 28, 30, 32, 33, 34, 35, 44, 151, 152, 159
Jones, W. D.: 184
Joplin Miners: 40, 42, 44
Kansas City Blues: 40, 42, 159
Kelley, Lynn: 44

Klier, Al: 153, 154, 160
Knoblauch, Charlie "Chuck": 77, 97, 98, 155, 156
Knoblauch, Chuck: 77
Knoblauch, Ed: 77
Knoblauch, Irwin: 77, 79, 155
Knothole Gang: 23, 25
Knox, Clifford "Bud": 75, 76, 77, 81, 129, 155
Kommy, Ray: 154, 155
Korach, Joe: 44
Kratzer, Duane "Dee": 35, 47, 152, 159, 161
Kreuger, Hans "Whitey": 81, 85, 87, 155, 160
Kruczyk, Tony: 77
KUOA radio station: 22, 26, 28
Kurkoski, Ed: 46
Lally, Tom: 161
Landis, Judge Kennesaw Mountain: 74, 75, 108, 185
Landthrip, Bill: 151
Laner, Monroe: 22, 40
Lawrence, Ray: 82, 155
Lawson, Dayton: 44
Ledbetter, Homer "Doc": vii, 7, 10, 11, 12, 32, 33, 36, 42, 45, 51, 64, 81, 128, 153
Lemarr, Jerry: 40
Lemke, Walter J.: 33, 35, 51, 53, 55, 81, 94, 95, 96, 100, 104, 121, 183, 185, 186, 187, 192
Lewis, Kermit: 57, 153, 159, 160
Lieb, Frederick G.: 117
Linch, Paul: 24, 25, 26, 30, 42, 151
Litzinger, Norm: 93
Lokotas, Steve: 153
Lollar, Sherman: 55, 81, 86, 103, 110, 168
Long, Huey: 38
Louis, Joe: 80
Love, Jack: 36

Luby, Steve: 82, 155, 160
Ludwig, Bob: 153
Luke, Raymond: 111
Lunsford, Tom: 10, 11
Lutz, Barney: 44, 46, 47, 54, 60, 62, 69, 153, 154, 160, 185
MacPhail, Larry: 109, 116, 119, 187
Madden, Melvin: 77
Marr, Clifton A. "Runt": 40, 80, 86, 129
Marshall, R. U.: 108
Mathews, Frank: 3, 4, 5, 15, 21, 22, 128, 151
Maus, Henry: 26, 27
Mayer, Ted: 60, 129, 154
McAllister, A. D.: 25, 46, 55, 110
McCarron, Bob: 62, 69, 154, 185
McCarty, Gene: 56, 153
McClain, Bill: 108, 115, 116
McGill, Tom: 5, 128
McRoy, Jerome: 40
McWhorter, Walter: 42
Meyer, Ken "Buddy": 62, 69, 185
Mhoon, Raymond: 7
Middle Atlantic League: 102, 111
Midland: 67
Milani, Frank: 154
Million, Robert: 48
minor leagues: viii, 38, 120, 173, 184
  expansion: xi
  levels of: vii
Monett Red Birds: 29, 40, 41, 42, 44, 45, 46, 48, 49, 50, 51, 52, 53, 55, 56, 57, 59, 62, 63, 64, 65, 66, 67, 68, 70, 71, 75, 77, 78, 80, 81, 82, 83, 85, 86, 87, 88, 89, 90, 91, 92, 93, 94, 96, 97, 98, 101, 102, 103, 108, 109, 128, 129, 153, 154, 155, 156, 157, 159, 160, 161, 162,

165, 168, 171, 172, 173
Moore, Herb: 10, 129, 157, 186
Moran, Cyril "Butch": 82, 83, 155, 159, 160, 161
Morgan, Charles: 82, 83, 155, 159, 160, 161
Morris, Hershel: 83
Morris, J. Walter: 4, 5
Morton, W. C. "Pete": 22, 186
Mosier, Russell: 10, 151
Mueller, Clarence "Heinie": 75, 83, 129, 171
Mullen, Vincent "Moon": 75, 80, 129
Munding, Andrew: 40
Murray, Dick: 30, 33
Murray, Johnny (Al): 47, 49, 52, 160, 161
Myers, Dale: 157
Nabor, Jake: 65
Narieka, Joe: 147, 161
Nasalik, Walt: 115, 157, 165
National Association of Professional Baseball Leagues (NAPBL): viii, ix, 4, 5, 17, 22, 38, 108, 109, 183, 192
Navarro, Augie: 68, 155
Naylor, Earl: 62, 69, 76, 77, 81, 83, 85, 154, 155, 163, 169, 185
Nebraska State League: 76, 88, 186
Nee, Johnny: 15
Needham, Troy: 44
Negri, Pete: 26, 42, 44, 46, 152
Neighbors, Bob: 50, 162, 169
Nelson, Walter: 71
Neosho Nighthawks: 61, 62, 63, 65, 66, 67, 68, 69, 70, 127, 129, 154, 159, 163
Neosho Yankees: 75, 78, 80, 81, 82, 83, 84, 85, 86, 87, 88, 89, 90, 92, 93, 94, 96, 97, 98, 99, 100, 101, 102, 103, 104, 108, 111, 112, 113, 114, 115, 116, 117, 127, 129, 131, 155, 156, 157, 159, 160, 161, 162, 163, 165
New Iberia: 67
New York Giants: 76
New York Yankees: 15, 42, 59, 63, 75, 93, 94, 108, 128, 129, 185
Nicely, Jim: 24, 29, 30, 32, 128, 151
Northeast Arkansas League: 187
Northwest Arkansas Times: vii, 2, 66, 76, 89, 100, 107, 14, 117, 185
Norton, Virgil: 14
Nowak, Walt: 77
Obenour, Jim: 161
Oceak, Frank: 90, 91, 93, 96, 102, 103, 104, 129, 156, 173
O'Connell, Ed: 49
Odneal, C. J.: 91
OK and Milady Cleaners: 60
Olson, Robert: 44, 54, 161, 185
Owen, Ansel: 155, 156, 160
Owen, Mickey: 168
Owens, Jesse: 53
Ozark Theatre: 101
Palace Theatre: iv, 77
Parker, Bonnie: 11
Parrott, Ray: 104, 156
Patterson, Lester "Pat": 75, 129
Paul, Jim: 156
Pavlich, John: 105, 156
Pennsylvania State Association: 11, 14, 32
Perryman, Curtis B.: 44
Peterlich, Eli: 161
Peterson, Lloyd: 157
Pittsburgh Pirates: 74, 75, 76, 89, 108, 129, 170
Playfair, Bob: 98, 157, 160, 161
Ponca City Angels: 61, 76
Pony League: 186
Poole, Ike: vii, 63, 64

Poole, Russell: 9, 10, 12, 13, 16, 17
Porter, Carl: 71
Poss, Elmer: 62, 185
Post, Wiley: 38
Powell, Ray "Rabbit": 22, 45, 56, 128, 129, 152, 153, 154
Prater, Ralph: 111, 116, 147, 187
Priddy, Gerry: 63, 154, 169
Prylich, "Farmer" Joe: 112, 113, 114, 115, 116, 147, 157, 165, 186
Ptak, V. James: 4, 86, 90, 108, 110
Purvis, Melvin: 31
Radabaugh, Ralph: 32, 33
Radokovich, Dan: 155
Raper, Clint: 34, 36, 49, 52, 54, 57, 153, 160, 161, 162
Richardson, Glen: 77
Rickey, Branch: viii, ix, 74, 82
Rinckey, Lawson: 29, 30, 44, 46
Robello, Al: 13, 19
Roberts, "Chief" Frisco: 157
Roberts, Howard: 152, 159
Rock, Les: 57, 153, 170
Rogers Apple Knockers: 8, 11
Rogers Cardinals: 24, 25, 26, 27, 28, 29, 30, 31, 32, 33, 34, 35, 36, 37, 40, 42, 127, 128
Rogers Lions: 45, 46, 48, 49, 50, 51, 52, 53, 54, 55, 56, 57, 59, 60, 61, 63, 65, 66, 67, 68, 69, 70, 71, 72, 127, 128, 129, 131, 151
Rogers Reds: 75, 76, 78, 79, 80, 81, 82, 83, 84, 85, 86, 87, 89, 127, 128, 129
Rogers Rustlers: 11, 12, 13, 14, 20, 22, 24, 127, 128
Rogers, George: 40
Rogers, Will: vii, 38
Roosevelt, Franklin Delano: 49, 59
Rorie, Ike: 30

Rucker, Paul: 26, 29, 30, 33, 71
Rush, George: 186
Rushing, Parker: 7, 10, 11, 17, 19, 24, 26, 30, 31, 157, 175
Russo, Caesar "Skee": 116, 157, 186
Ruth, Babe: 81
Rutledge, Kenneth: 82, 162
Sakovich, Mike: 156
Sams, Tony: 153, 154, 159
Sarver, Bill: 156, 160
Schmeling, Max: 80
Schwab, Melvin: 77, 85, 155
Scott, Douglas: 10, 16, 151
Scott, Randolph: 101
Seal, Bill: 77, 81, 82, 84, 151
Seaman, Lloyd Milton: 44
Seamster, Bernal: 22, 39, 40, 41, 44, 59, 60, 61, 73, 81, 90, 185
Seamster, Jess: 5
Seligman (MO): 4, 17
Serpa, Lindy: 160
Sertich, Mike: 86, 129, 155
Shaughnessy playoff system: 59
Shaw, Clifford: 5, 14
Shoals, Leo "Muscle": 185
Sigafoos, Frank: 83, 85, 172
Sileber, Joe: 155
Siloam Springs Buffaloes: 7, 9, 10, 12, 13, 14, 15, 16, 17, 18, 127, 128, 151
Siloam Springs Cardinals: 108, 109, 110, 111, 112, 113, 114, 115, 116, 117, 127, 128, 157
Siloam Springs Travelers: 25, 26, 28, 30, 31, 32, 33, 34, 35, 36, 37, 40, 43, 45, 46, 47, 49, 50, 51, 52, 53, 54, 56, 57, 58, 59, 61, 62, 63, 65, 66, 67, 68, 69, 70, 71, 75, 76, 77, 78, 80, 81, 82, 83, 84, 85, 86, 87, 89, 152, 153, 154, 155, 156
Smiley Park: 24, 46

Sinay, Andy: 69, 71, 152, 153, 154, 185
Six, Ora: 92
Skidgel, Jim: 187
Skidgel, Leon: 80, 85, 155, 161, 162, 165
Smalling, Earl: 54, 153, 154, 155
Smith, Dave: 53
Smith, Ed: 65, 68, 69, 78, 96, 98, 154, 165
Sonneman, W. F.: 101
Southeastern League: 110
Southern Association: 76, 183
Springdale (AR): 4, 5, 7, 17, 21, 40, 53, 60
Springfield Cardinals: 20, 21, 35, 40, 41, 45
St. Louis Browns: 59, 75, 89, 102, 108, 129
St. Louis Cardinals: viii, 20, 22, 28, 35, 43, 58, 73, 74, 75, 82, 108, 128, 129, 185
Stapleton, Frank "Buck": 51, 56, 128, 152
Stebe, Clifford: 91, 98, 102, 104, 156
Stice, Marc: 7, 22
Streets, Don: 44
Strunk, Ray: 160
Swartzman, Alton: 157
Szuch, Joe: 93, 103, 104, 156
Tahlequah (OK): 21
Tarrant, Claude: 154
Texas League: 183
Thomas, Allan: 10, 13, 24, 26, 32, 34, 42, 151, 152
Toenes, W. Harrel "Hal": 160, 161
Tone, Rudolph "Woody": 52, 153, 159, 160
Tonnsen, Mel: 153, 154
Toomes, Harry "Hal": 155
Trewhitt, C. W.: 40
Troupe, Jack: 69, 154
Tuck, Herman: 22, 40
Tucker, Thurman "Joe E.": 134
Turner, Ben: 152, 160
Twibell, Rex: 157
Twin Ports League: 183
Tyson, Cecil "Turkey": 185
Van Wey, Jim: 62, 65, 66
VanSickel, Cliff: 160
Villipique, Ace: 35, 152, 158, 162
Vinita, Oklahoma: 16, 28, 60, 61, 62, 73, 127, 129
Vinson, Ernest: 11
Wagenhurst, Howard "Chick": 84, 85, 165
Ward, Hugh: 76
Ward, Walt: 66, 165
Washington Hotel: 114
Watkins, Earl "Inky": 76, 85, 86, 155
Watson, Cline: 7, 11, 14, 16, 53
Werner, Bill: 34, 128, 152, 153
Western Association: 3, 16, 22, 23, 32, 35, 40, 41, 42, 44, 45, 61, 173, 187
Western League: 3, 43, 45
West-Texas New Mexico League: 67
White, Albert: 31, 65, 67
White, Buck: 151
White, Doug: 26, 30, 42, 44, 46, 54, 80, 91, 152, 153, 185
White, J. W.: 14, 151
Wiegand, Don: 157
Williams, Al: 42
Williams, Harry: 81, 86, 91, 94, 155
Wills, Bob: 102
Wilson, "Red": 3, 5, 6, 128
Wilson, Charley: 23, 24, 128
Wilson, E. L.: 40
Wilson, Les: 10, 11, 13, 14, 23, 27,

29, 30, 32, 44, 46, 49, 54, 152,
153, 154, 155
Wollard, Herb: 12, 19, 165
Wolverton, Marv "Wimpy": 76,
155, 159, 160
Woodrow, Rudolph:
See Tone, Rudolph "Woody"
Young, Morris "Cy": 13
Young, Paul: 85, 93
Youngblood, LeRoy: 66, 165
Zielinski, Florian: 155

J.B. HOGAN is a prolific and award-winning author. He grew up in Fayetteville, Arkansas, but moved to Southern California in 1961 before entering the U. S. Air Force in 1964. After the military, he went back to college, receiving a Ph.D. in English from Arizona State University in 1979.

    J.B. has published over 300 stories and poems. His novels, *The Apostate, Living Behind Time, Losing Cotton,* and *Tin Hollow*, two short story collections entitled *Fallen* and *Bar Harbor,* and his book of poetry, *The Rubicon*—are available at Amazon, iBooks, Barnes & Noble, Books-A-Million, and Walmart.

www.ingramcontent.com/pod-product-compliance
Lightning Source LLC
LaVergne TN
LVHW041615070426
835507LV00008B/247